# MANDALAS FOR PEACE,
# FUN AND ART

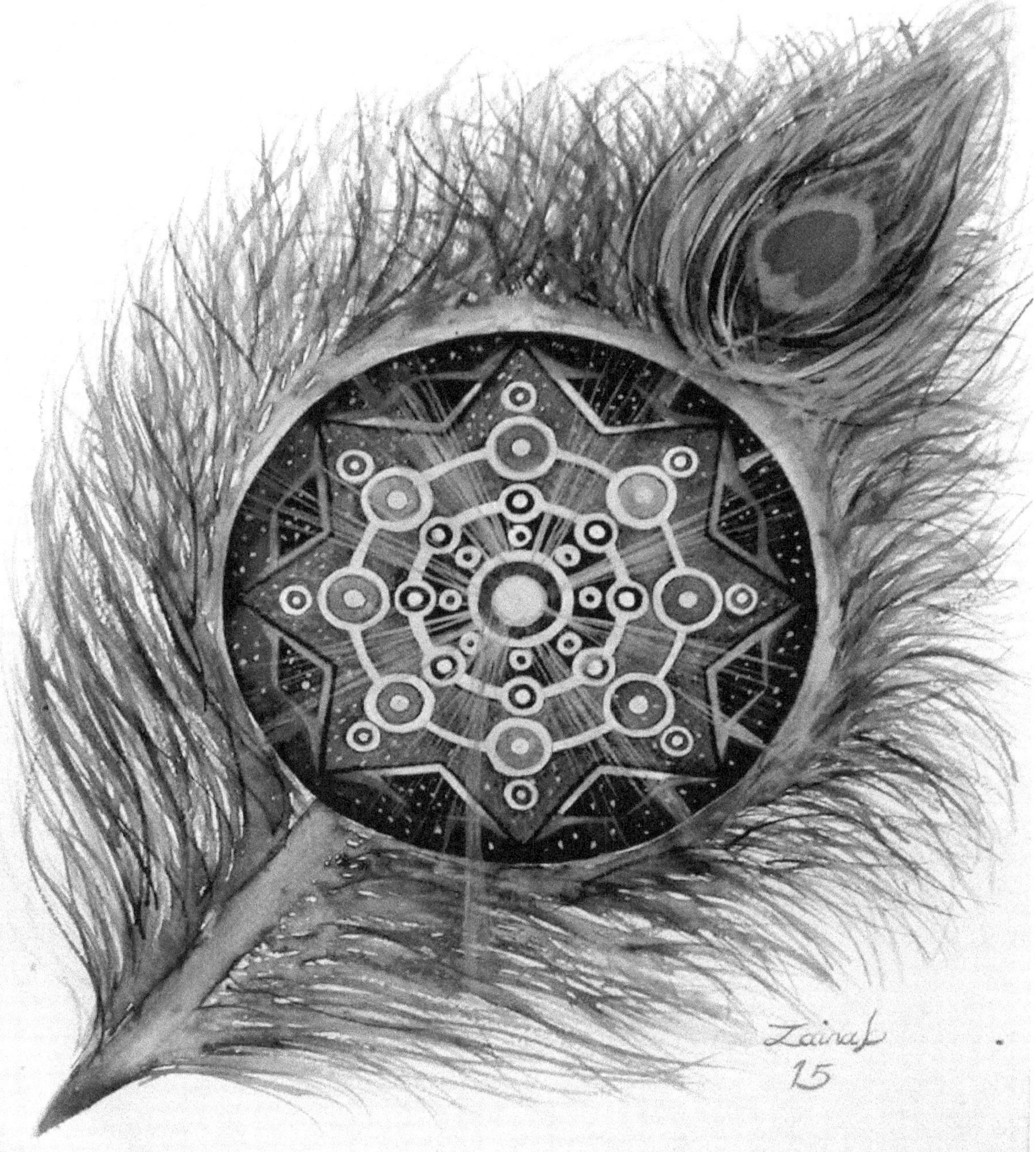

**Parsons**

Practicing mandalas not only heals the soul in a sort of meditation but it's also a joyful exercise that keeps artist's hand flexible for art work.

# Table of Contents

# Introduction

As a watercolor enthusiast and artist, I found out that practicing mandalas drawing and coloring not only heals the soul in a sort of meditation, but also gives a joyful exercise and keeps artist's hand flexible for art work and adds extra flexibility with practice.

For those young and adult art trainees, I recommended practicing mandalas for its artistic and peaceful benefits.

In this eBook, I'm collecting for you easy, medium and hard mandalas sketches for eastern and westerns mandalas design, that I used to copy into my canvas creating many different results, from one mandala base drawing, by using watercolors and little imagination.

Enjoy this peaceful artistic experience too either by coloring each mandala directly at the book or copying it into your canvas, so you can color with coloring pencils or normal watercolors and brushes.

**Zainab Alqadi**

Artist

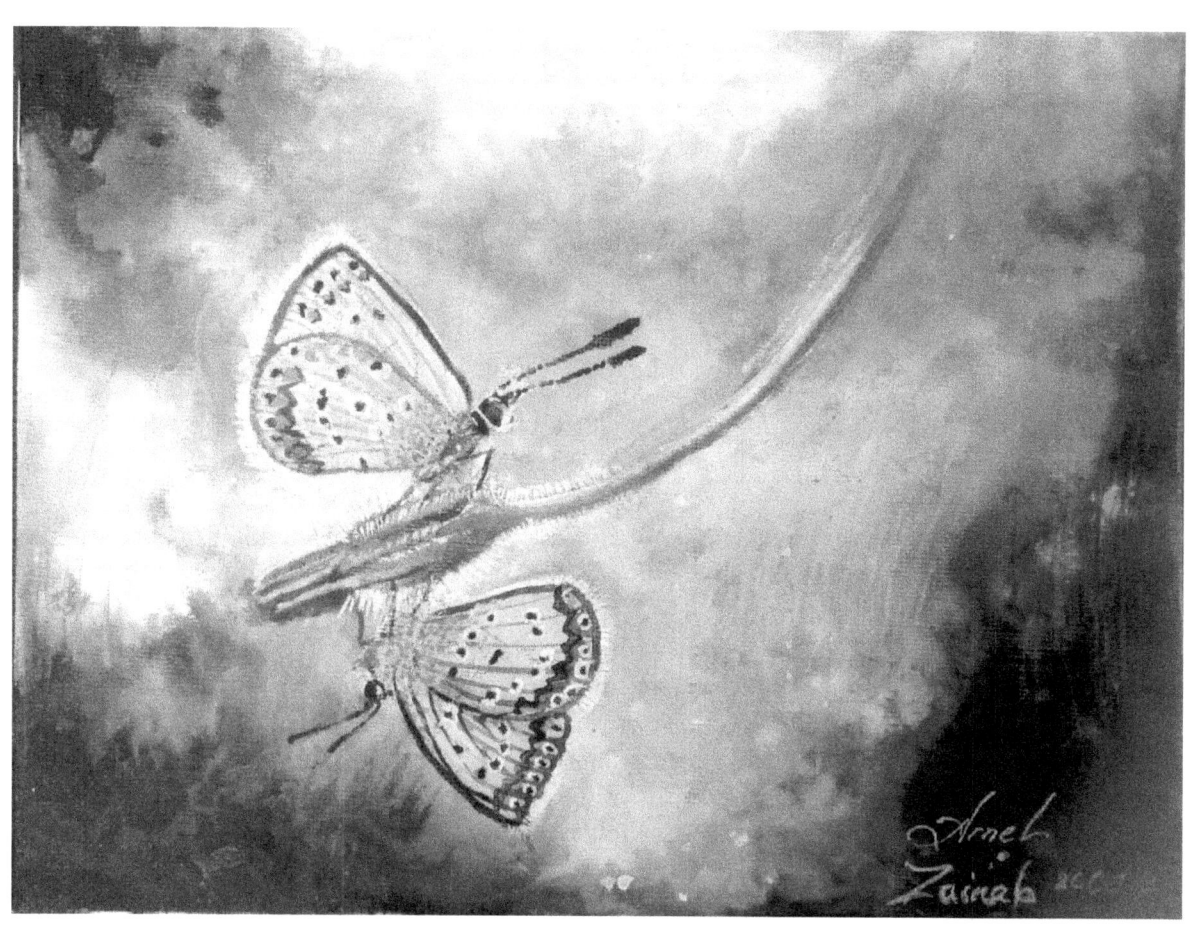

# Mandalas

**Mandala** (Sanskrit: *circle*) is a spiritual and ritual symbol in Indian religion, representing the universe. In common use, mandala has become a generic term for any diagram, chart or geometric pattern that represents the cosmos metaphysically or symbolically; a microcosm of the universe.

The basic form of most Mandalas is a square with four gates containing a circle with a center point with each gate in the general shape of a T. Mandalas often exhibit radial balance.

In various spiritual traditions, Mandalas may be employed for focusing attention of practitioners and adepts, as a spiritual guidance tool, for establishing a sacred space, and as an aid to meditation and trance induction.

Creating Mandalas helps stabilize, integrate, and re-order inner life.

According to the psychologist David Fontana, its symbolic nature can help one "to access progressively deeper levels of the unconscious, ultimately assisting the meditators to experience a mystical sense of oneness with the ultimate unity from which the cosmos in all its manifold forms arises.

Circle 1

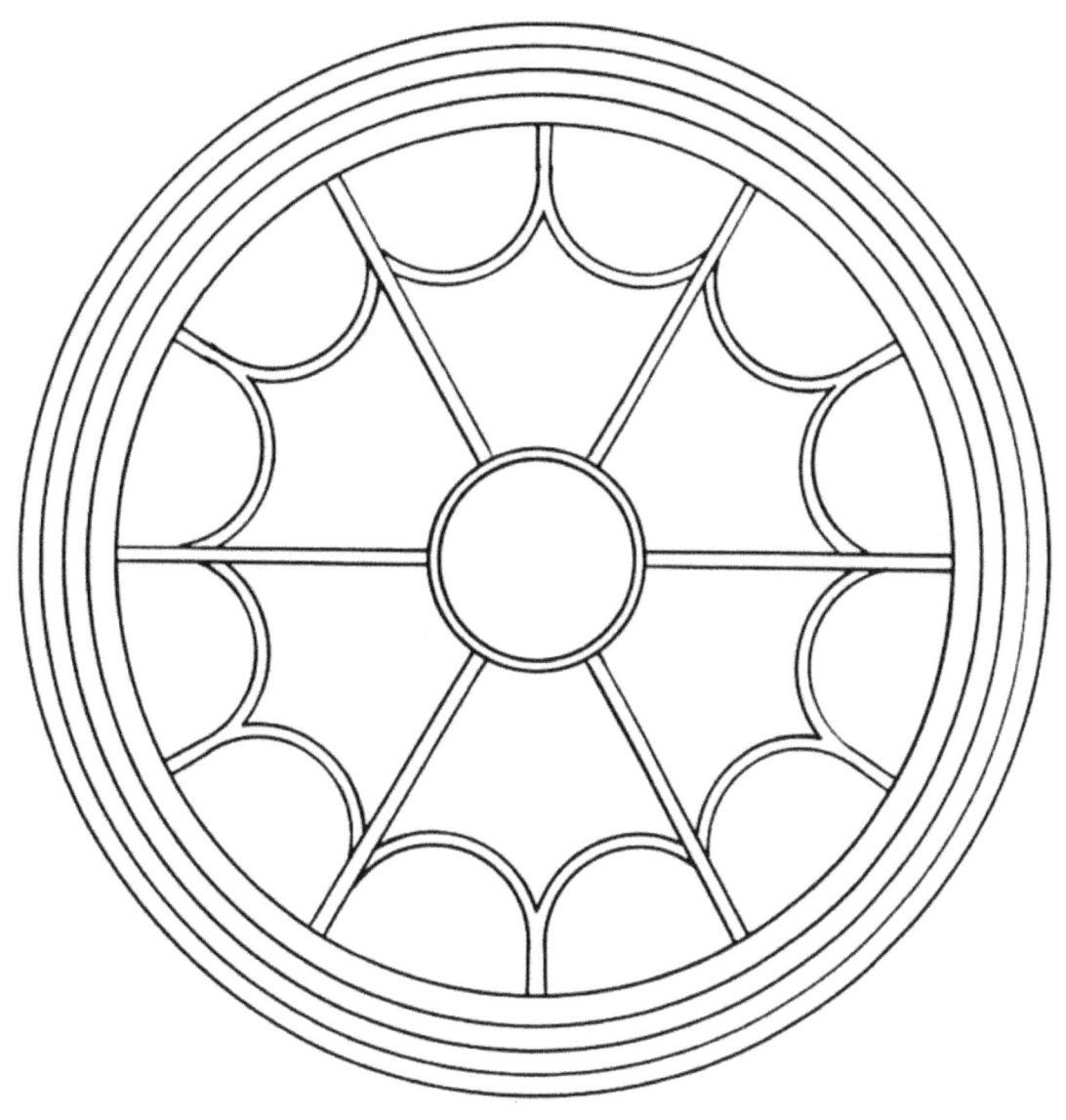

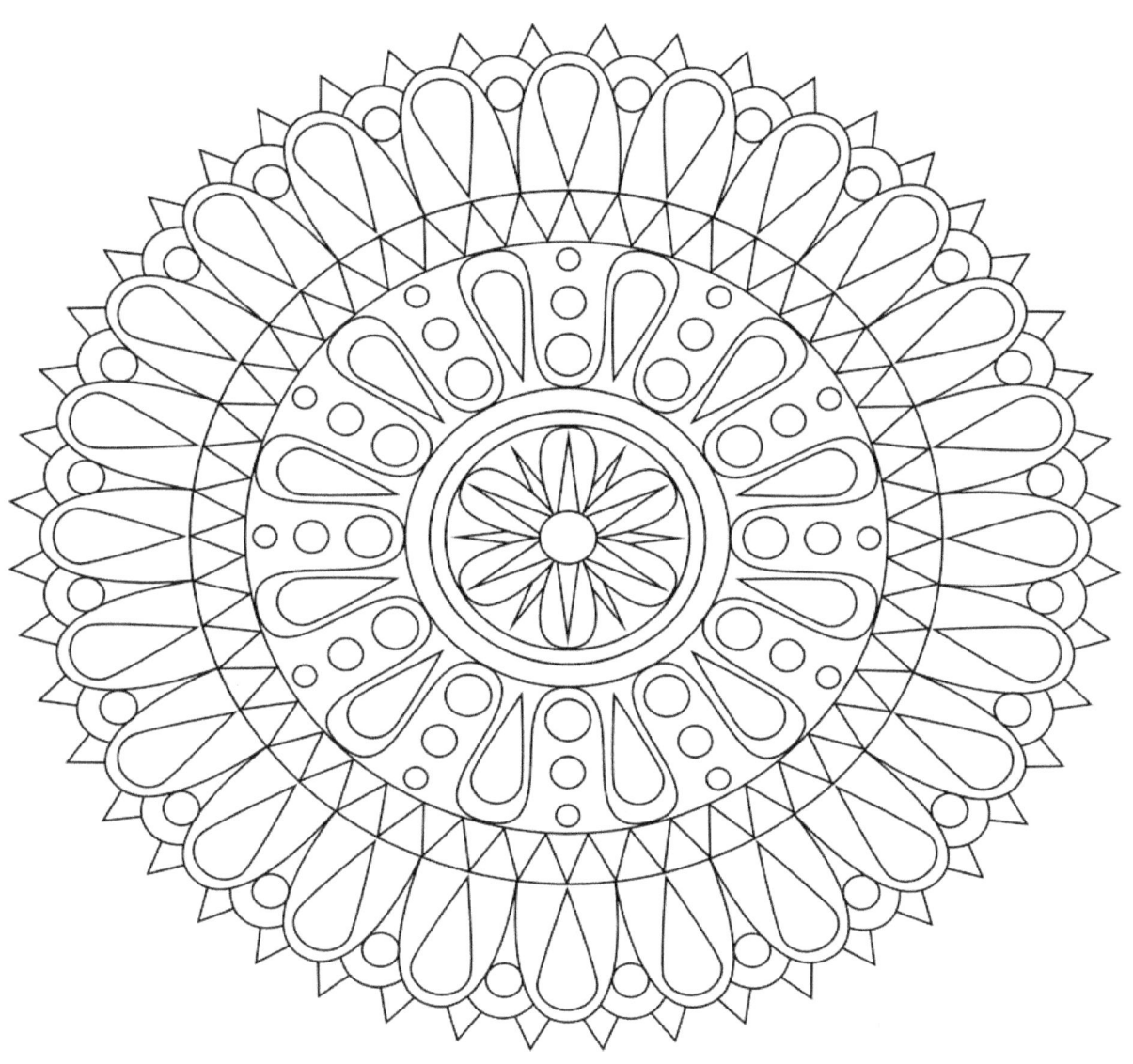

Circle 3

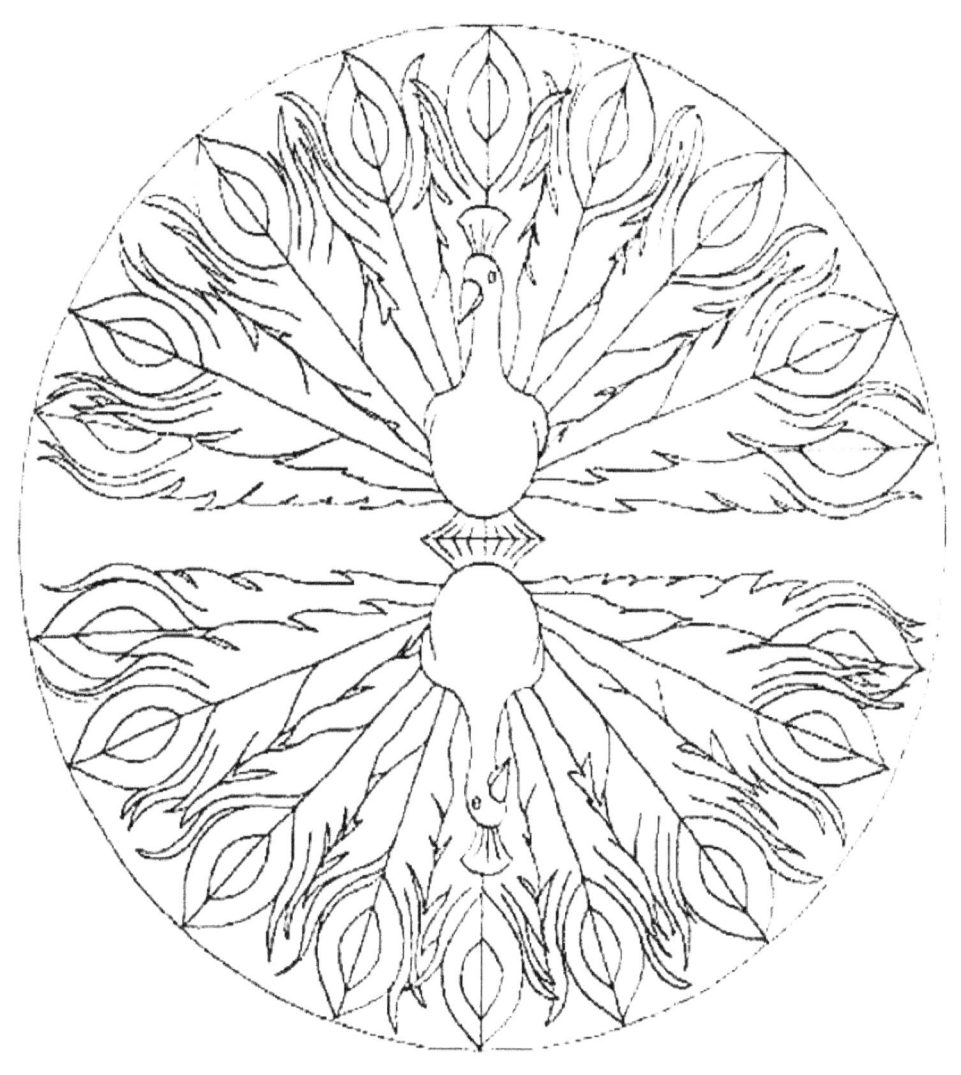

Cross 1

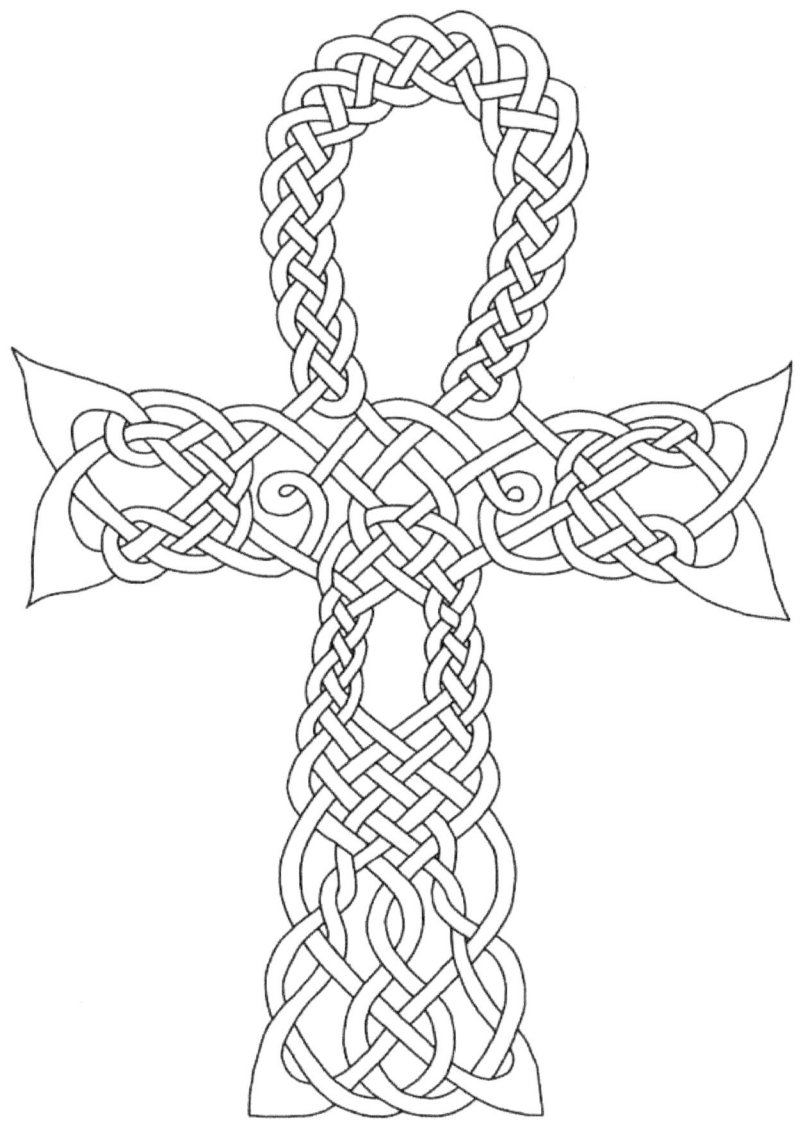

Circle 4

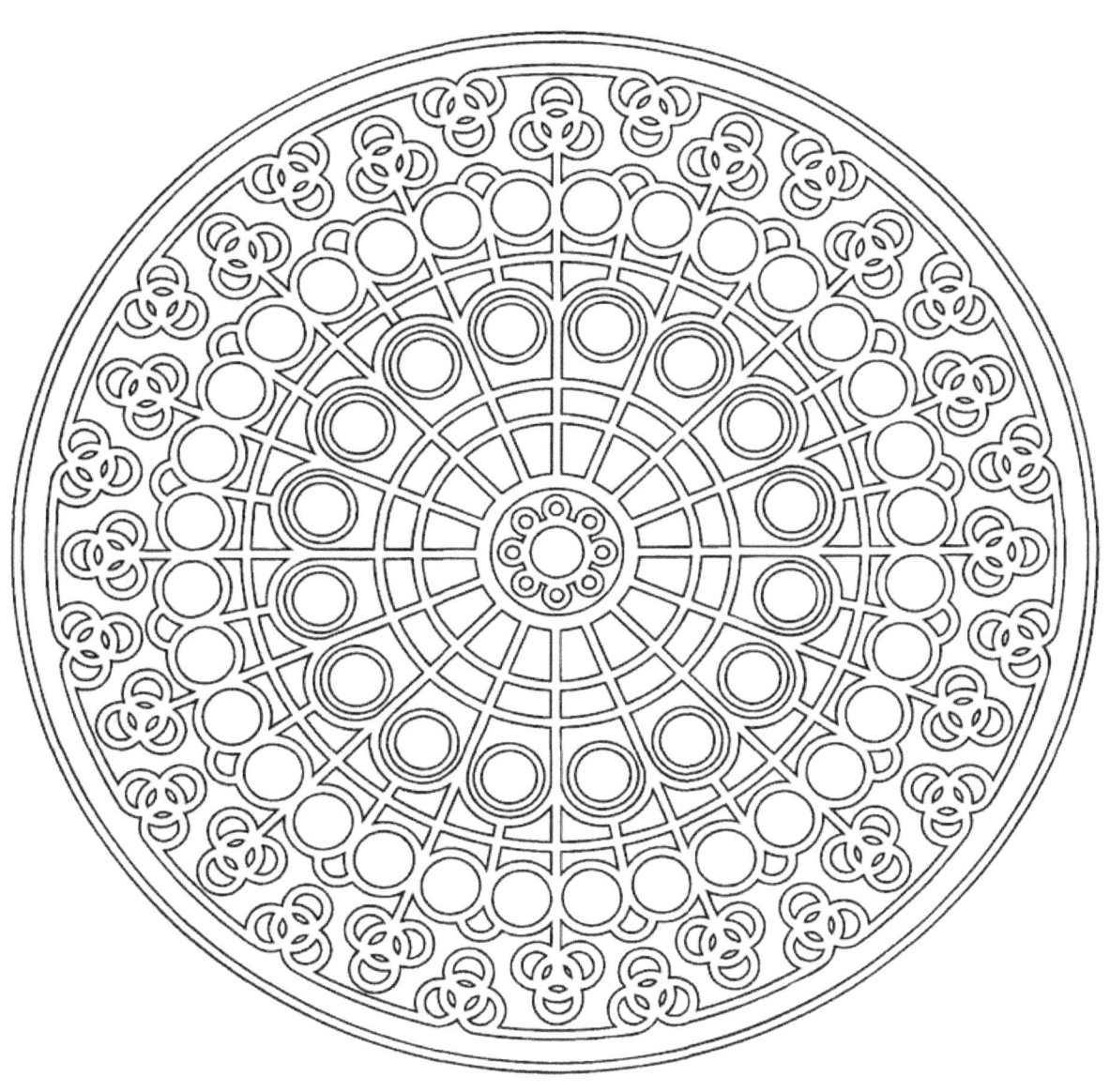

Star 1

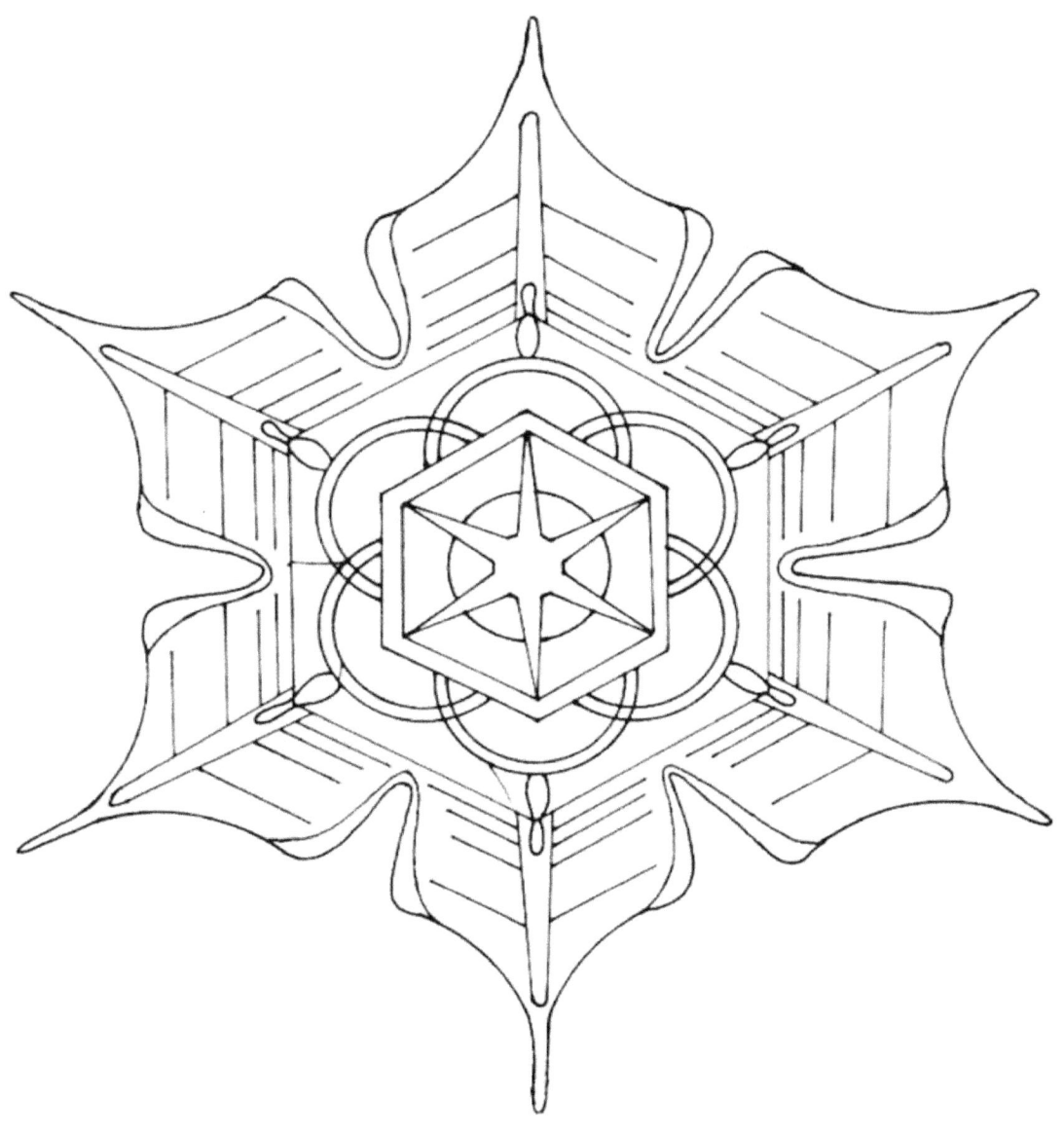

Circle 5

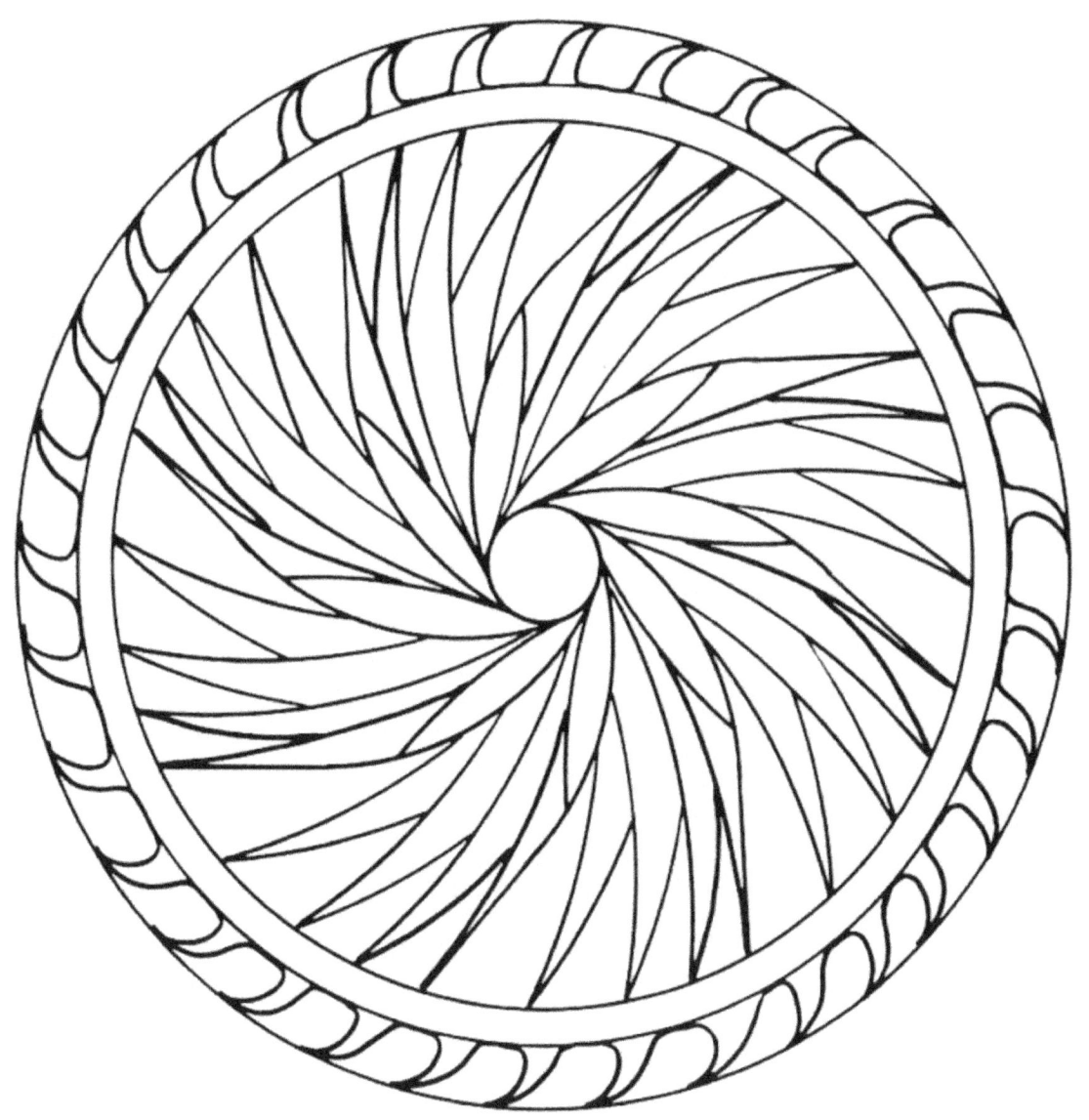

Circle 6

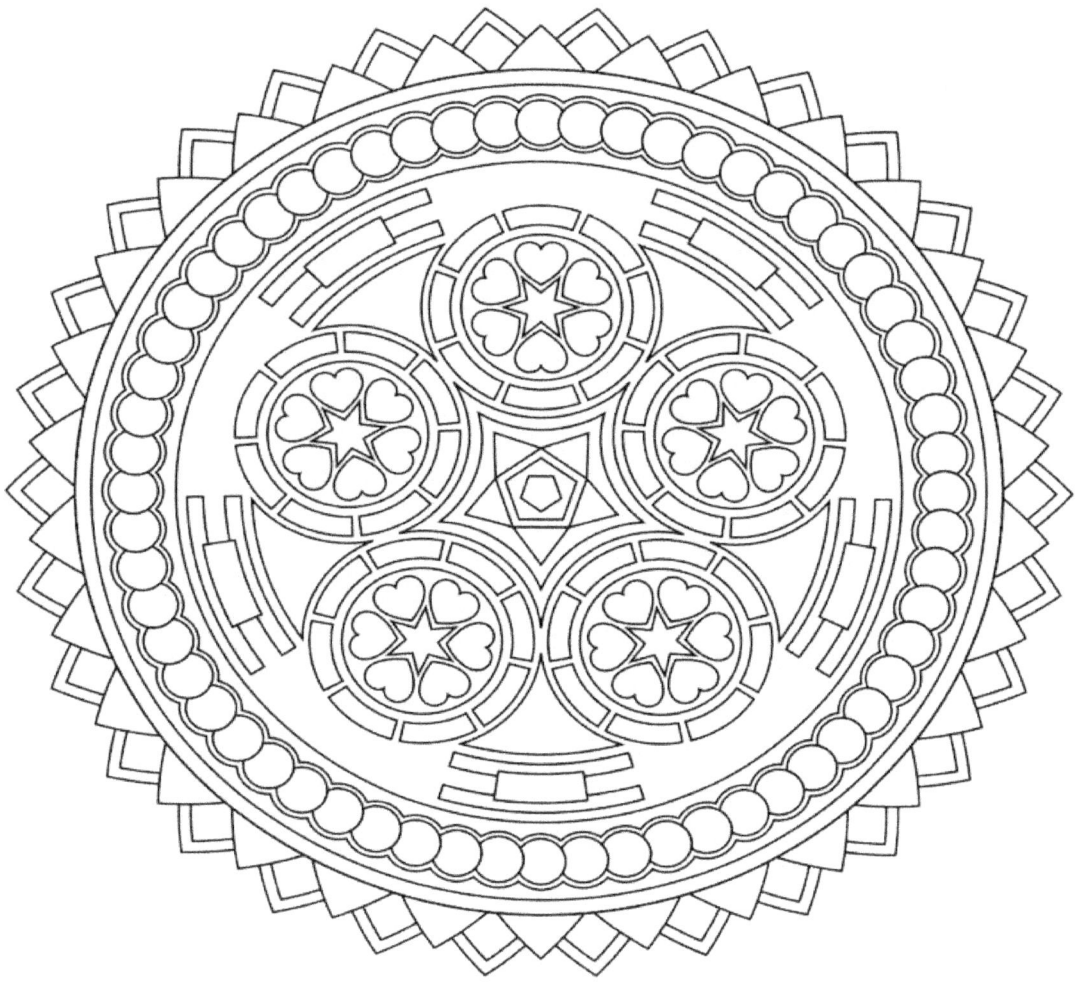

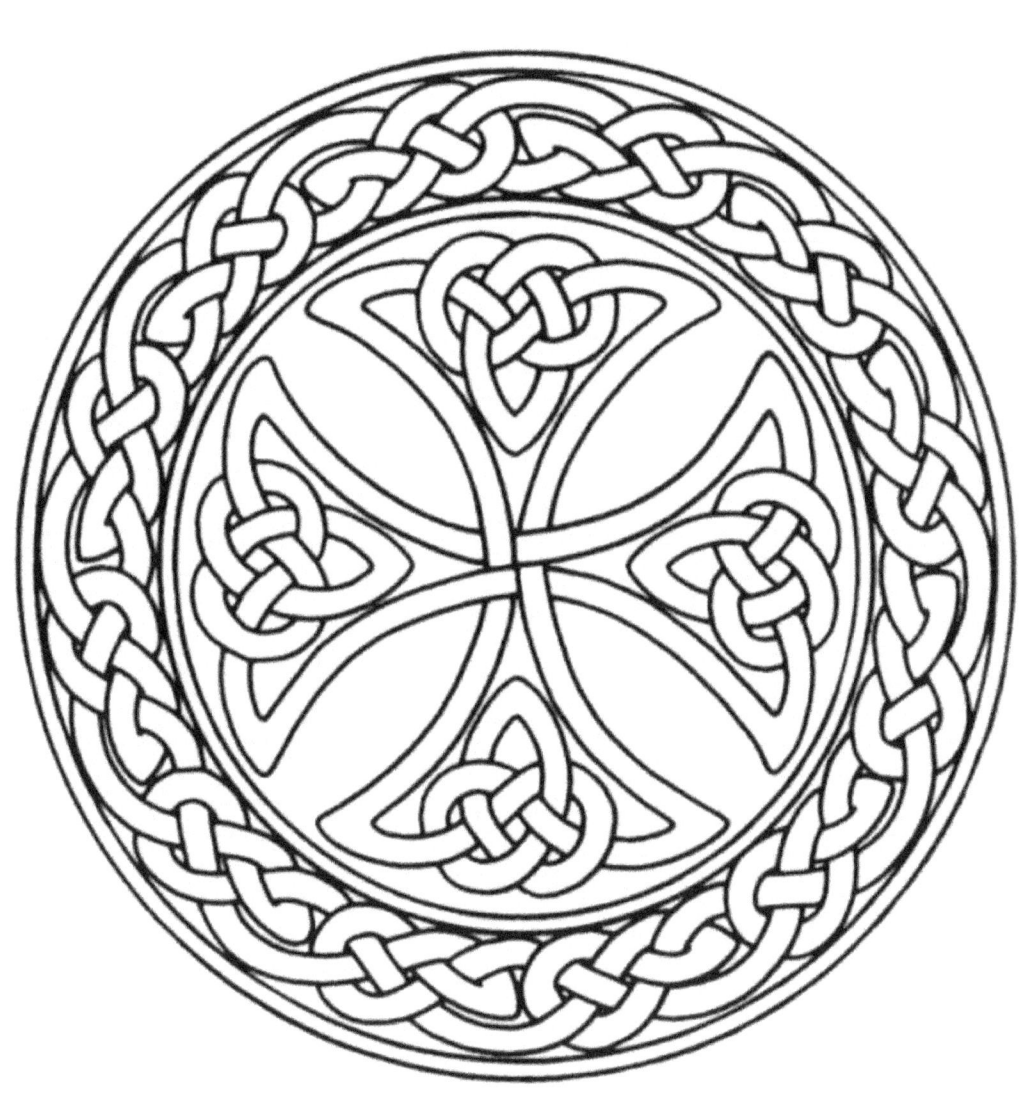

Star 2

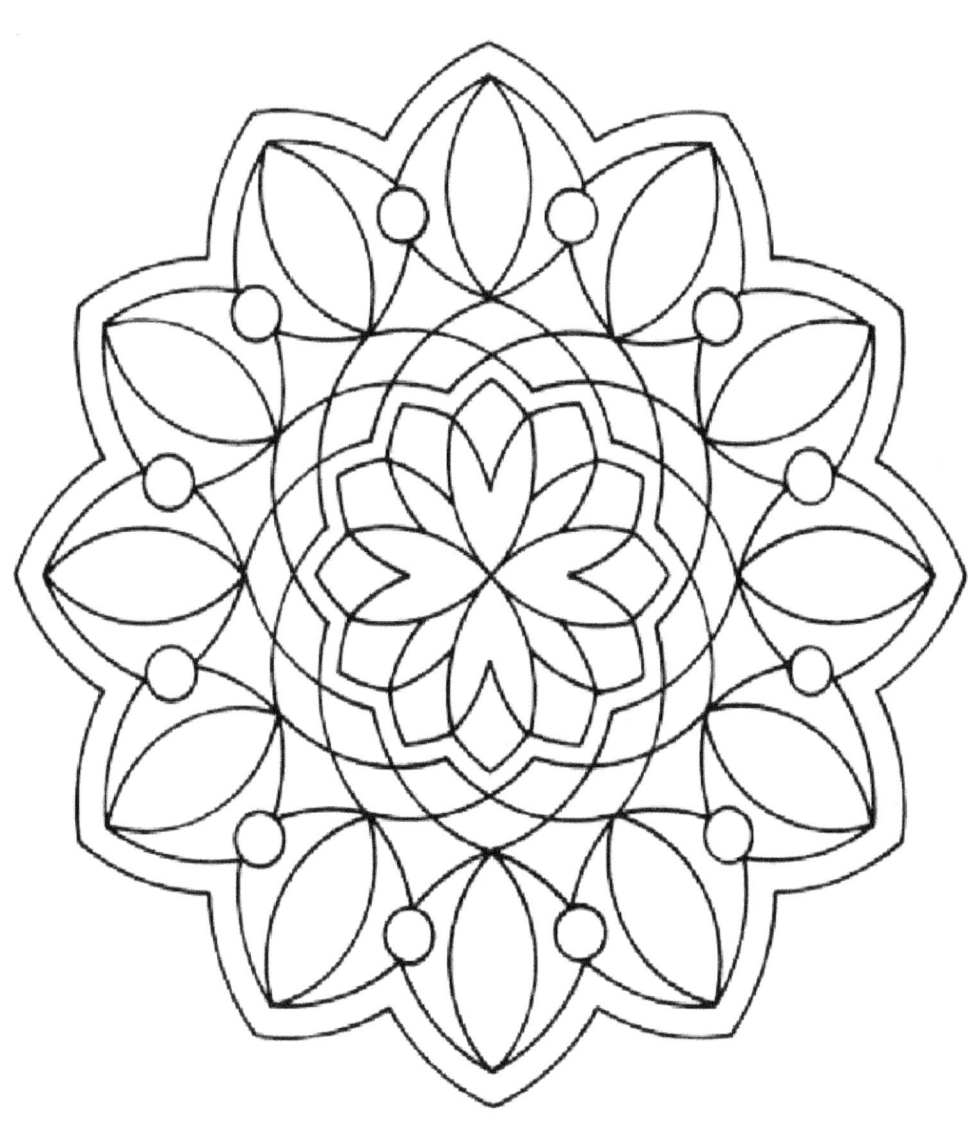

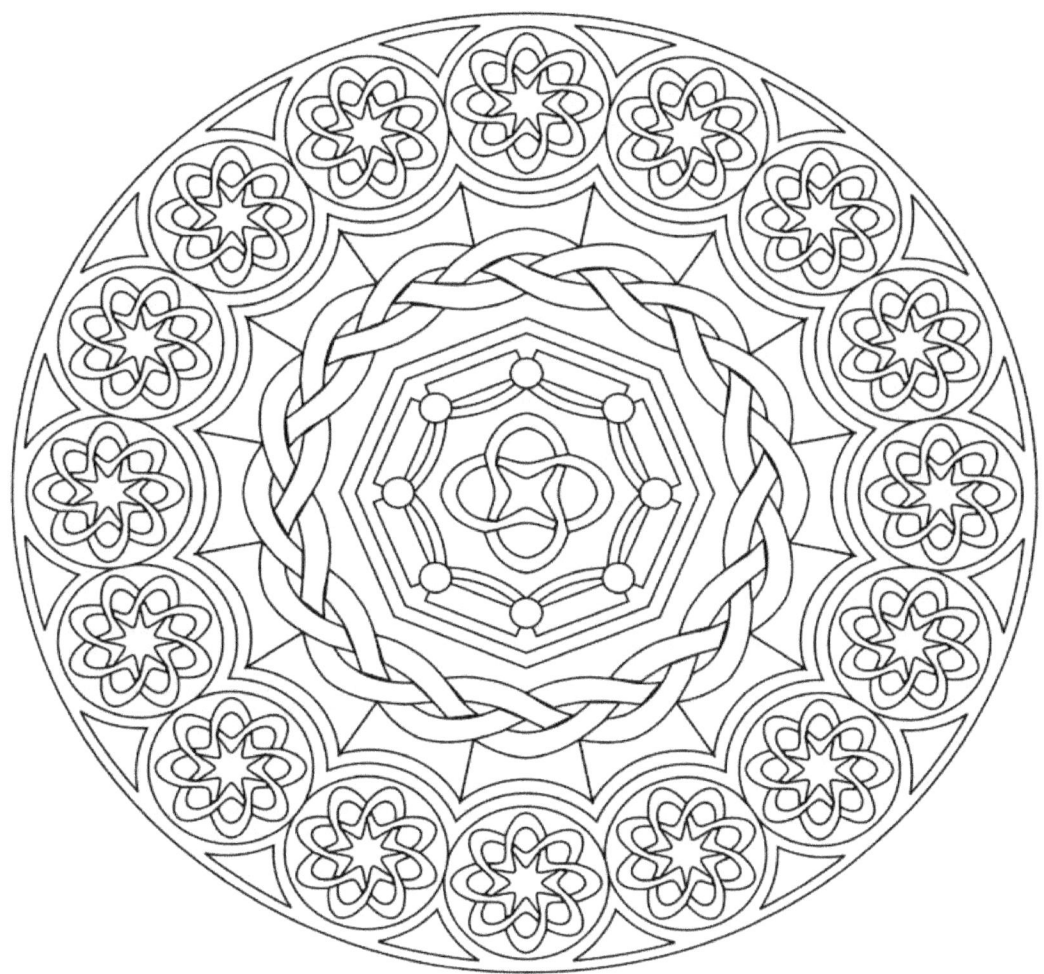

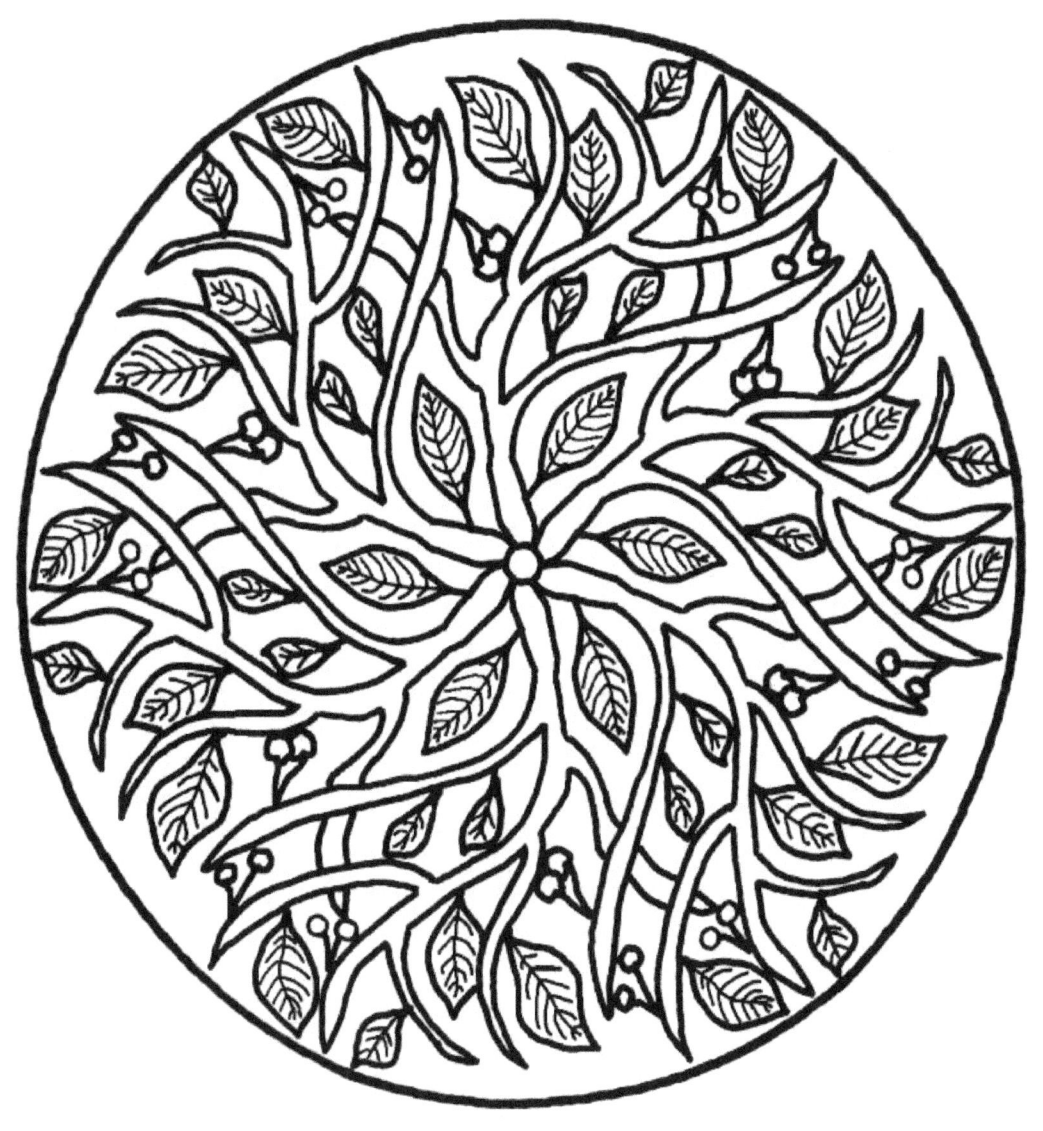

**Square 1**

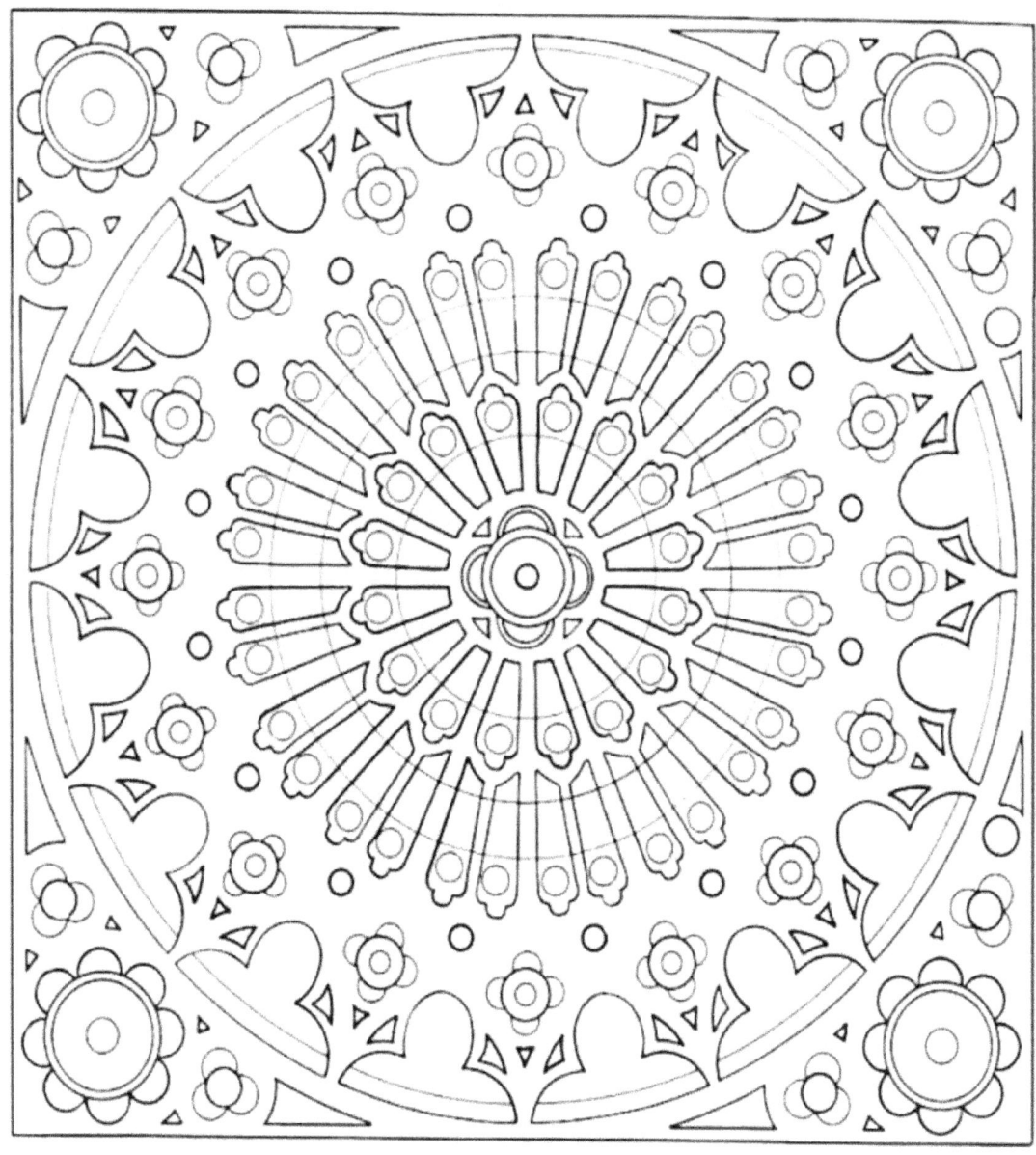

Circle 10

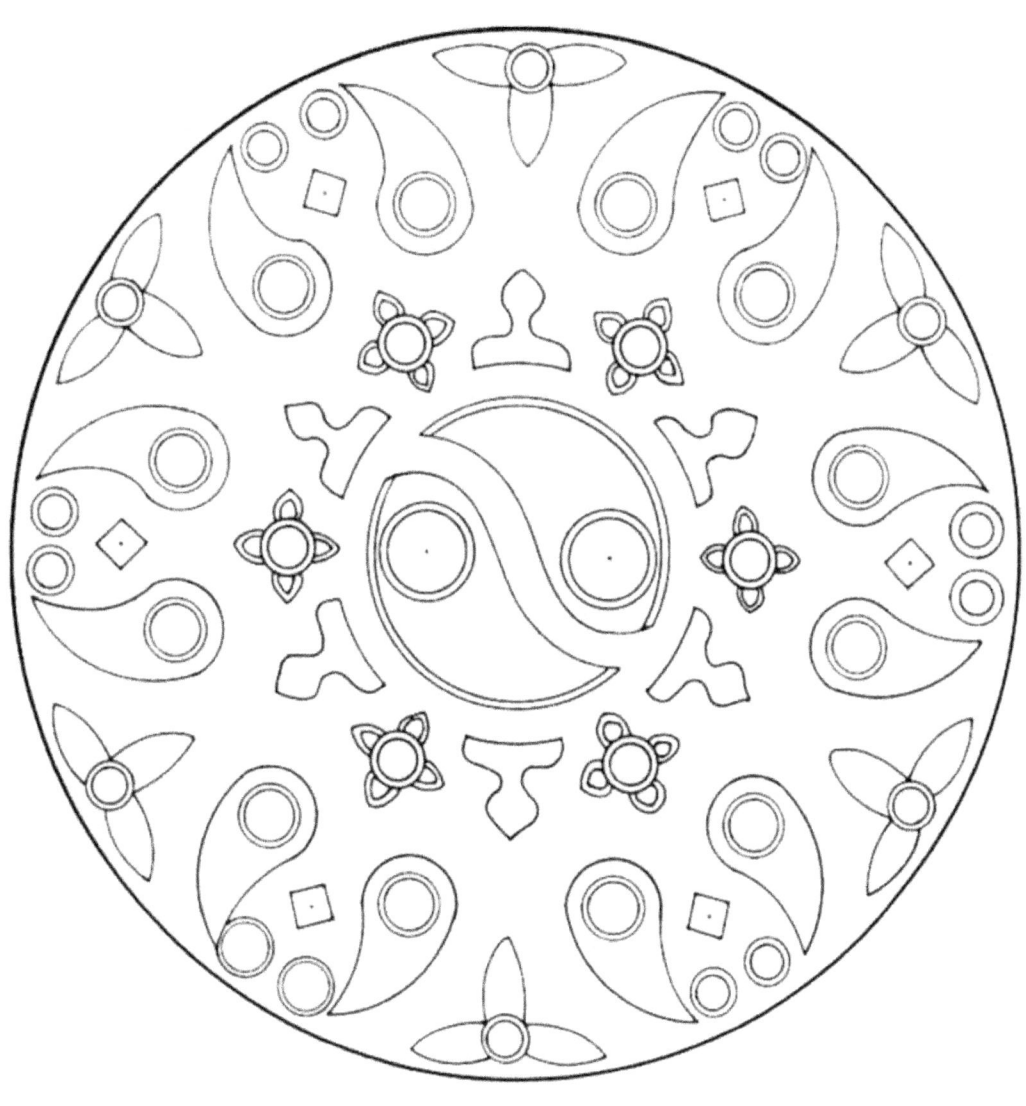

Circle 11

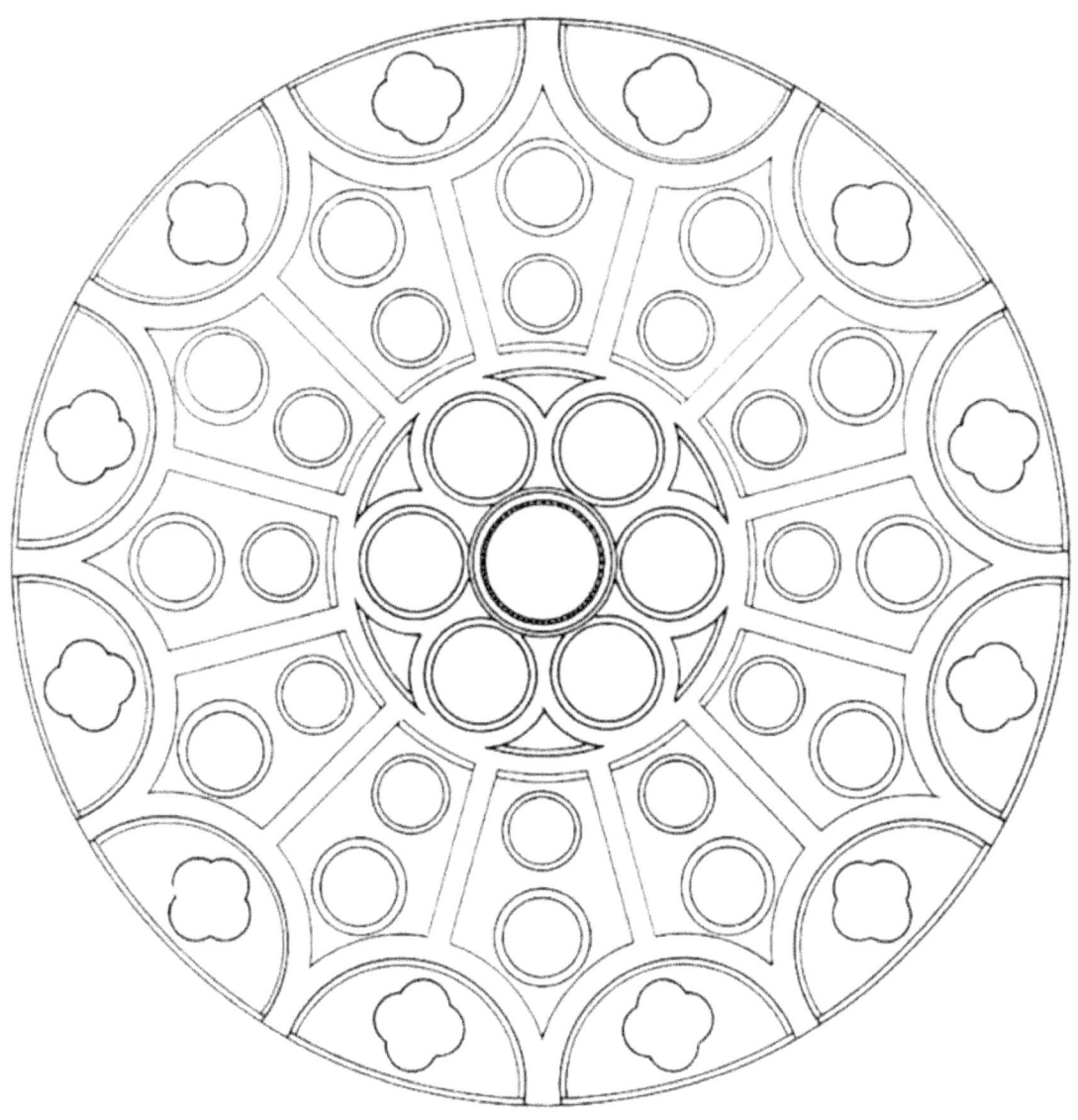

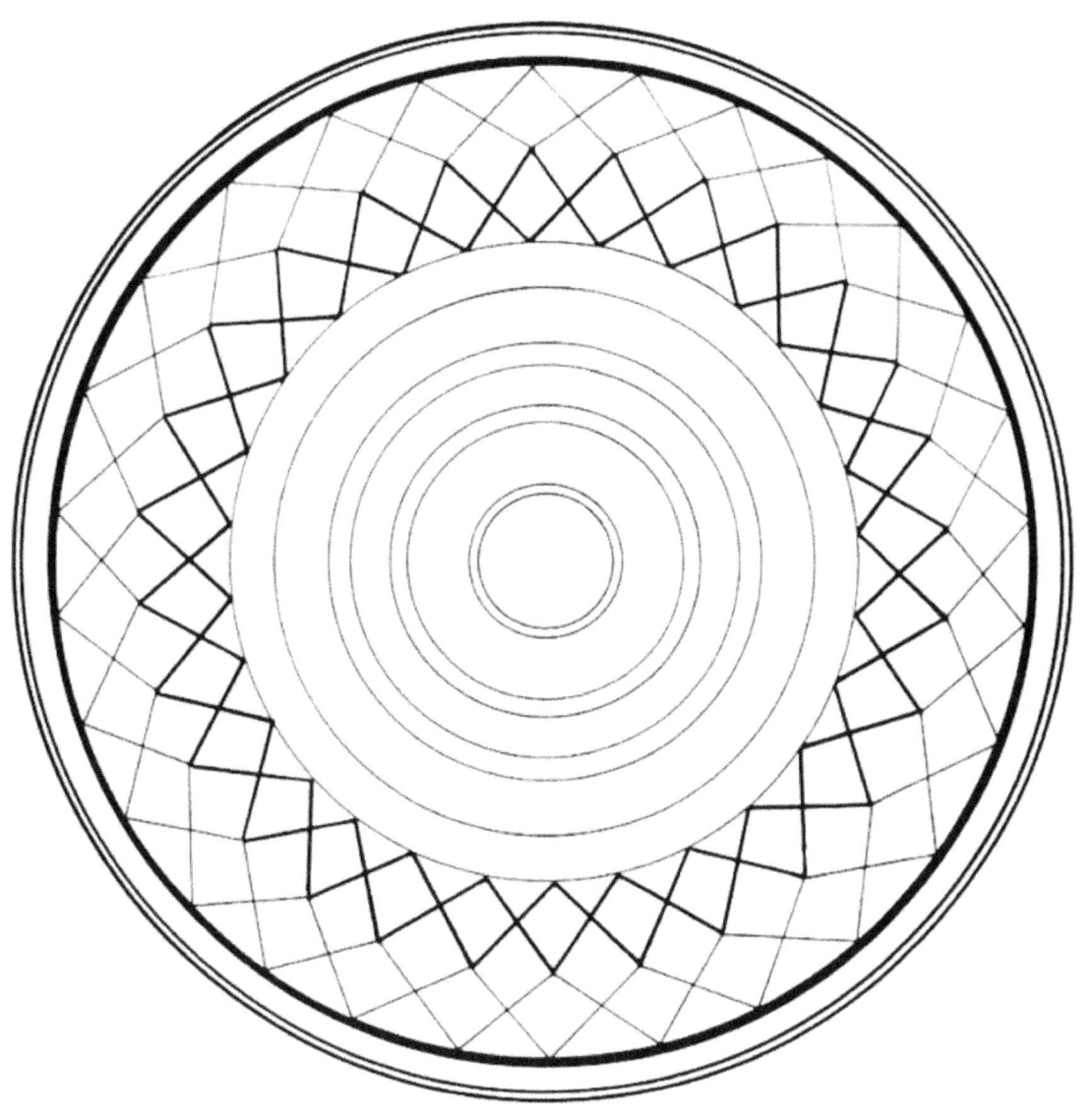

Circle 13

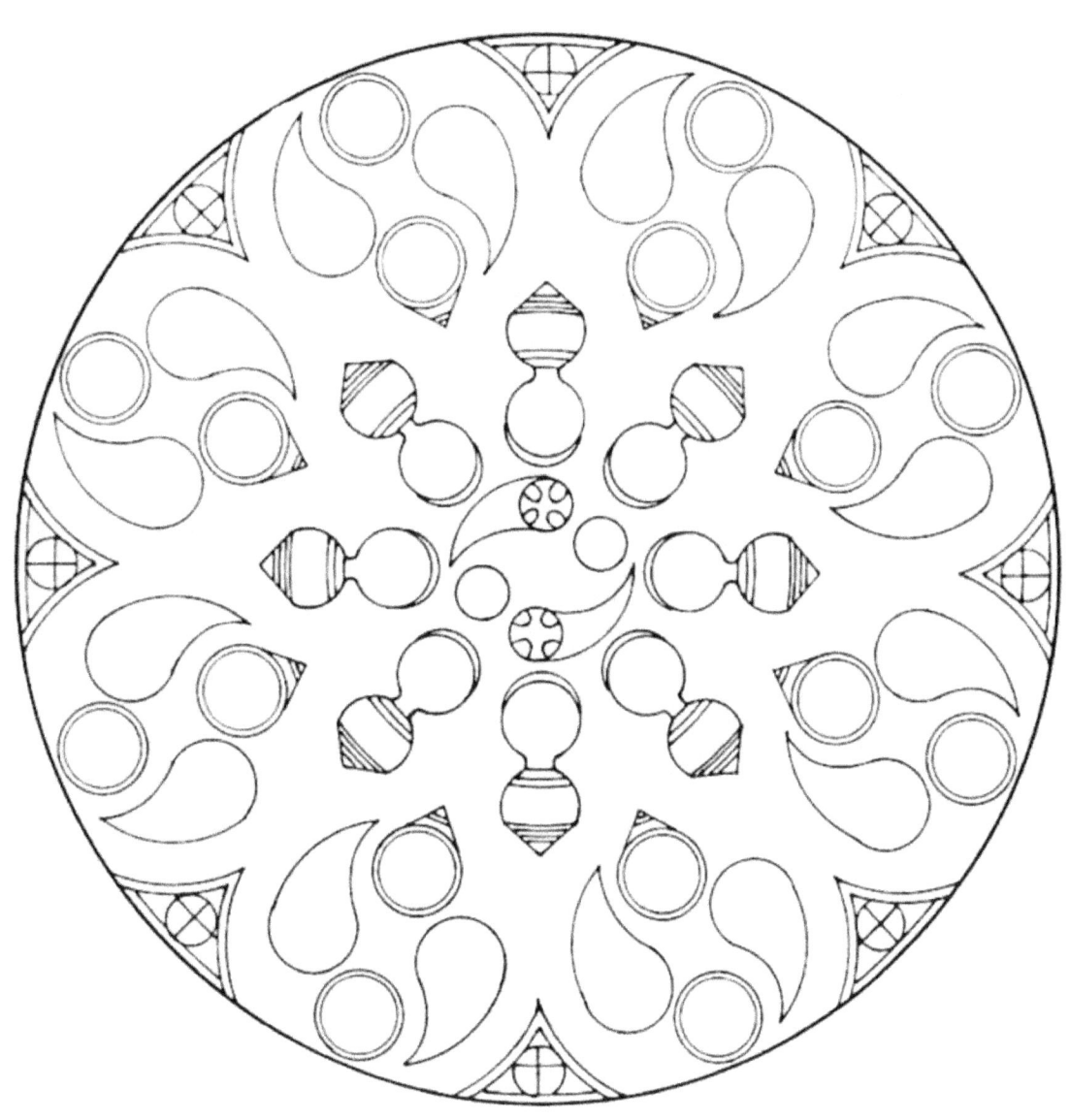

Circle 14

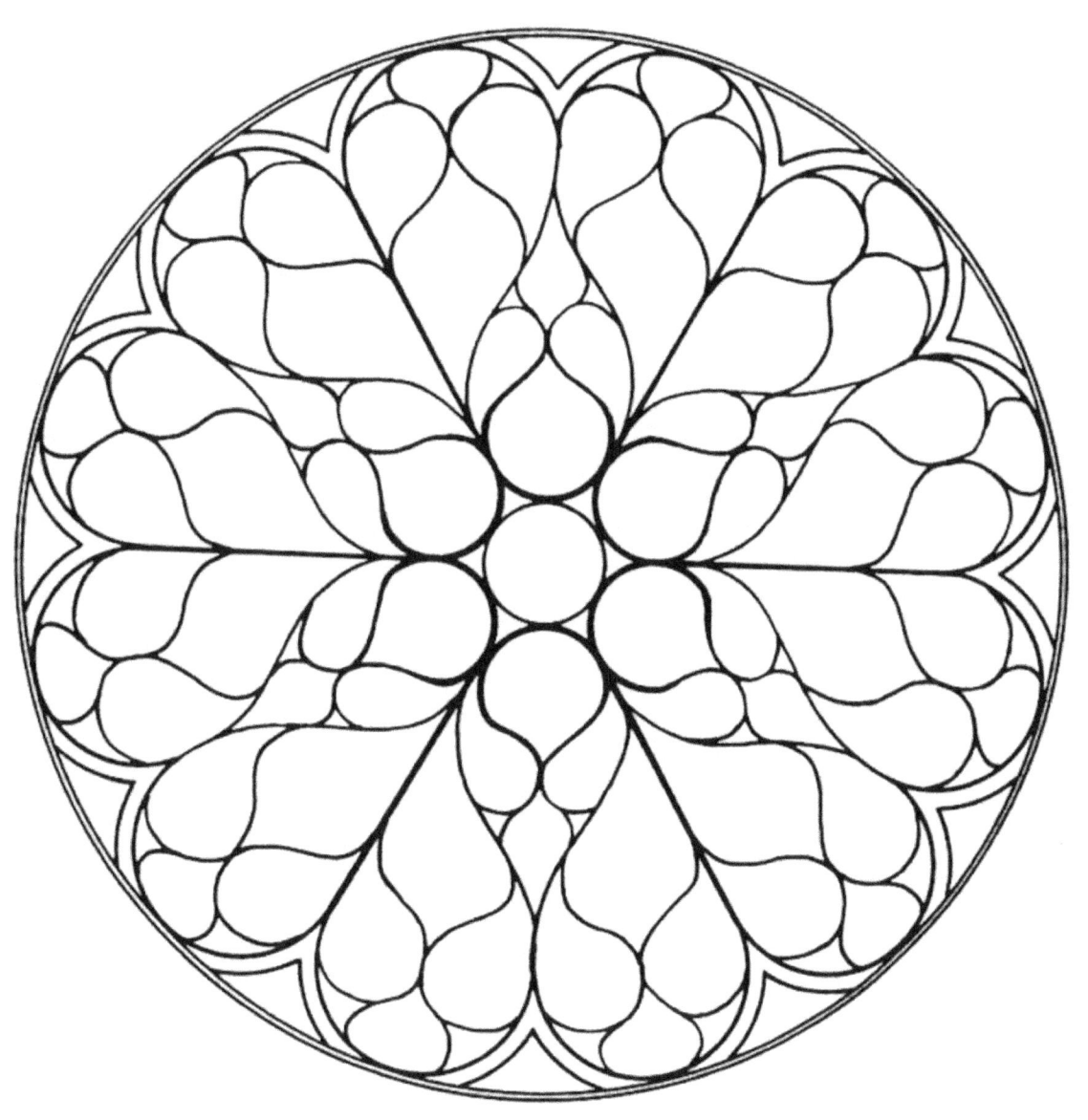

Circle 15

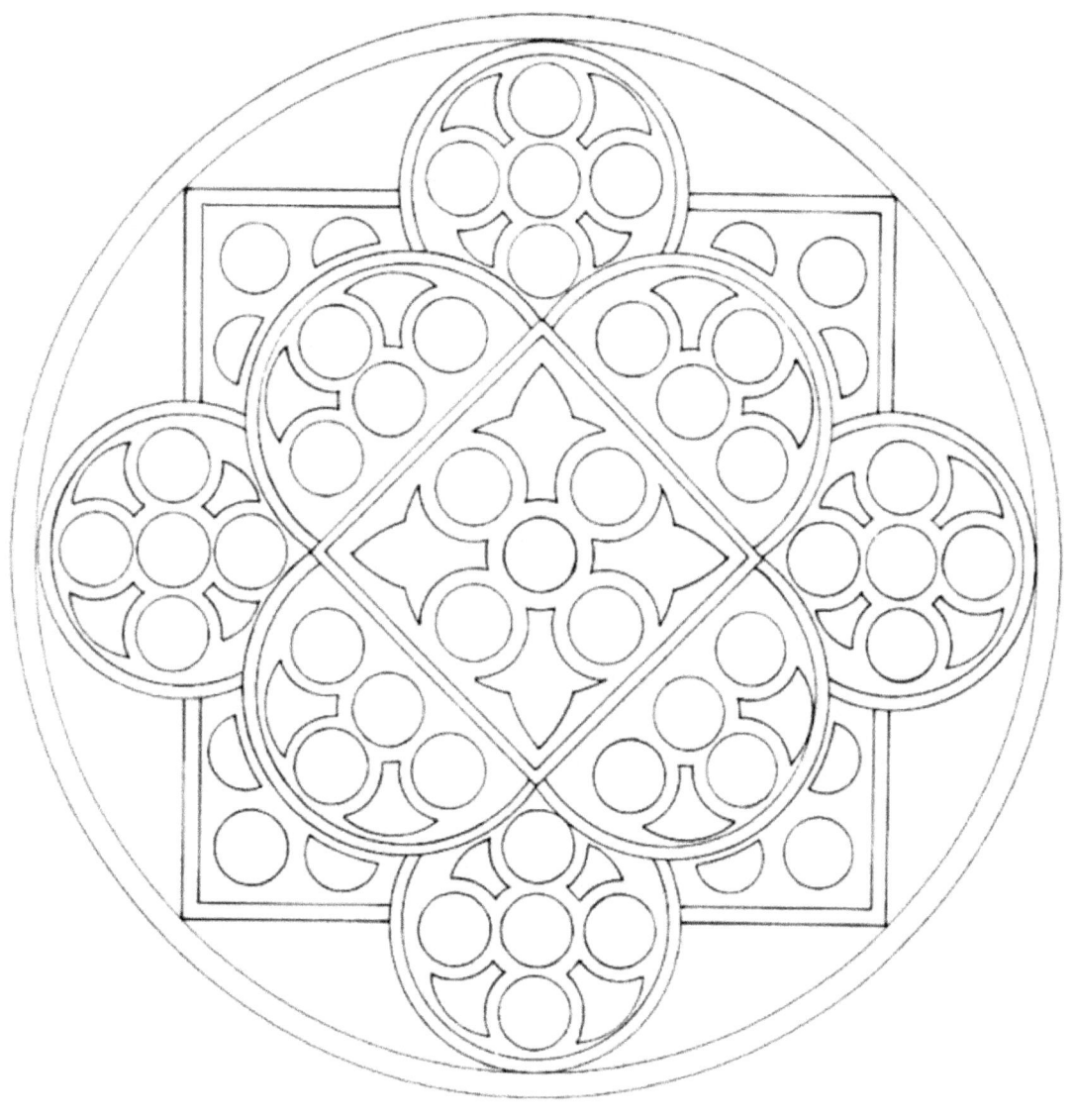

Circle 16

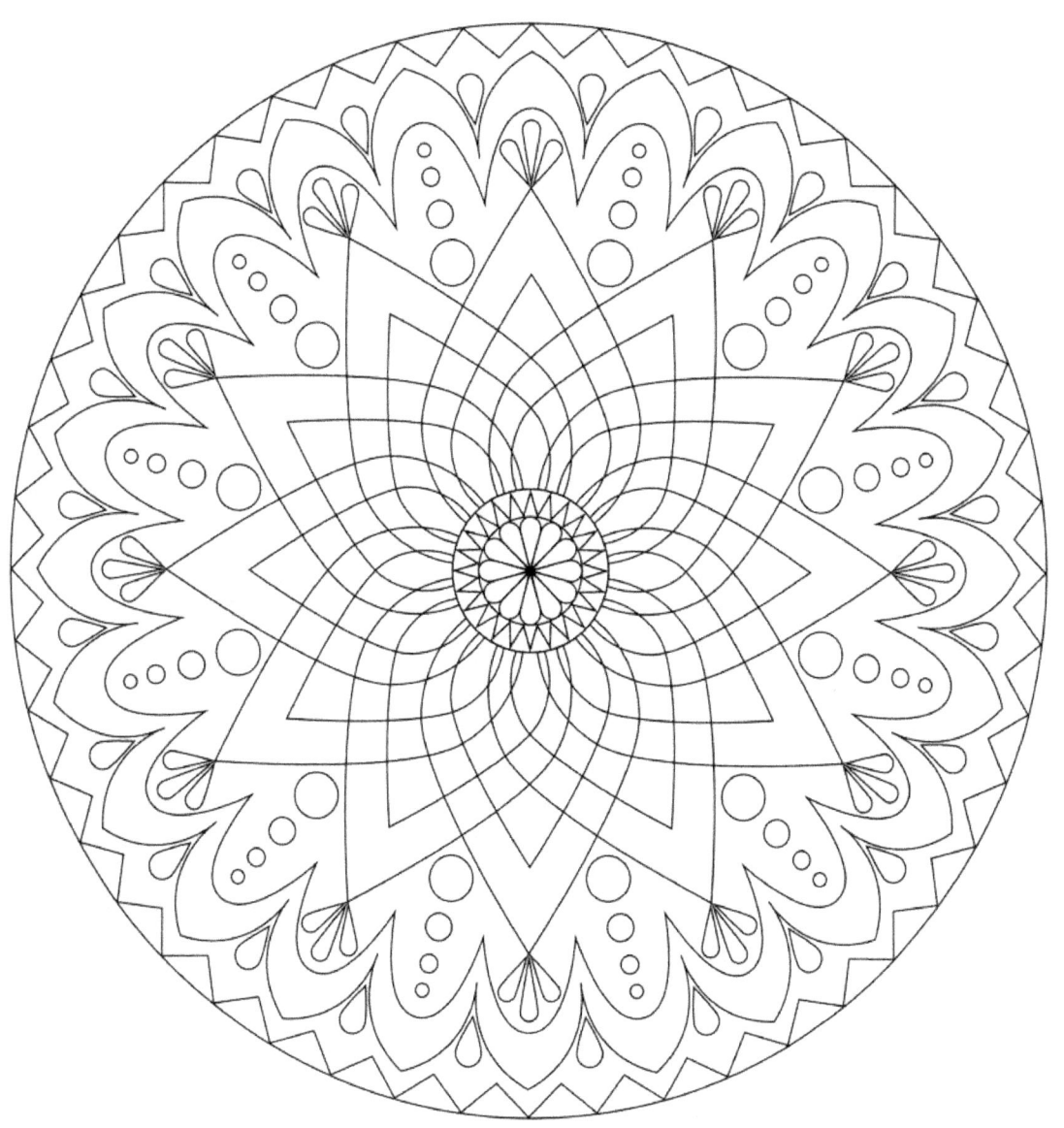

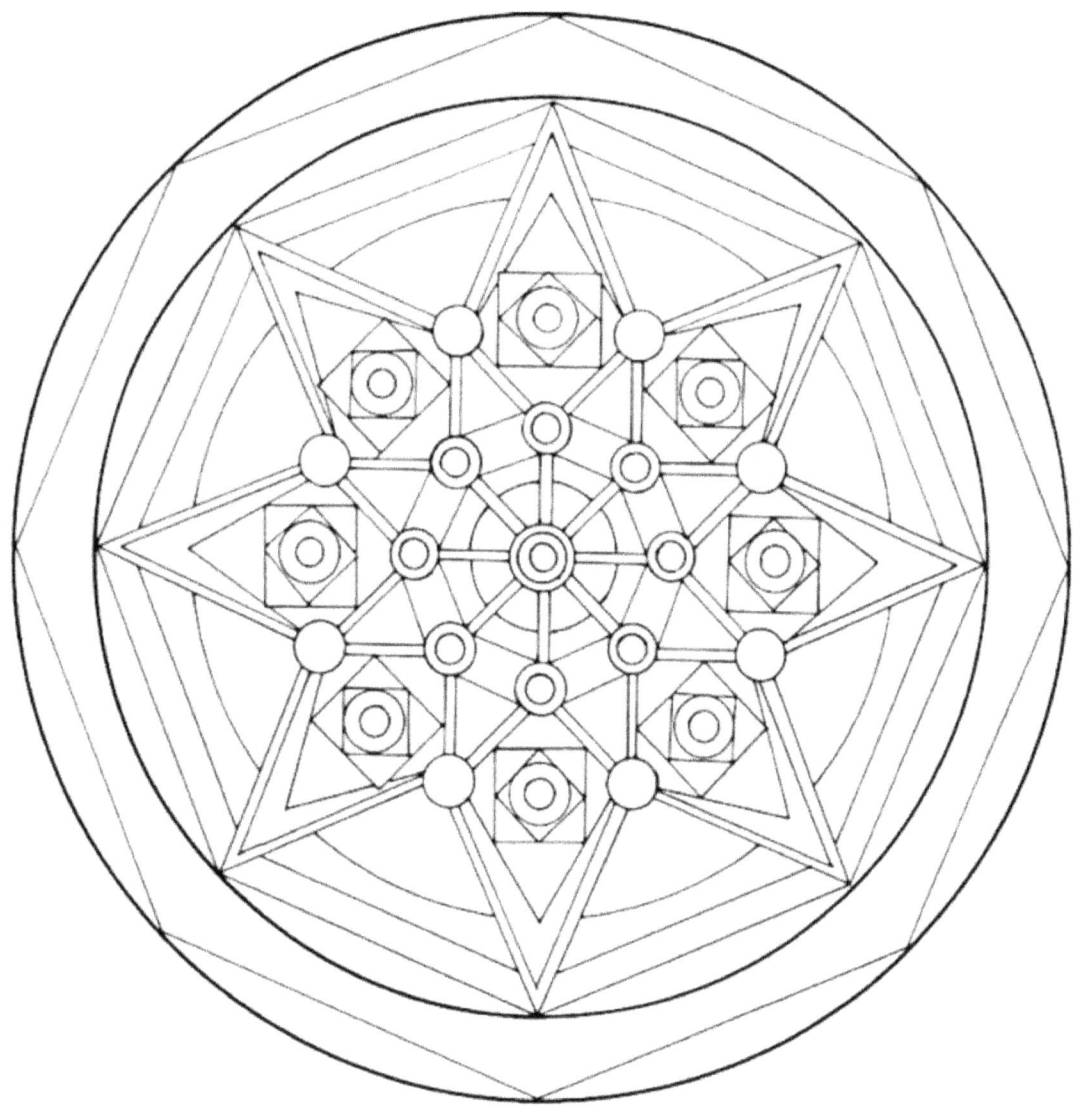

Circle 18

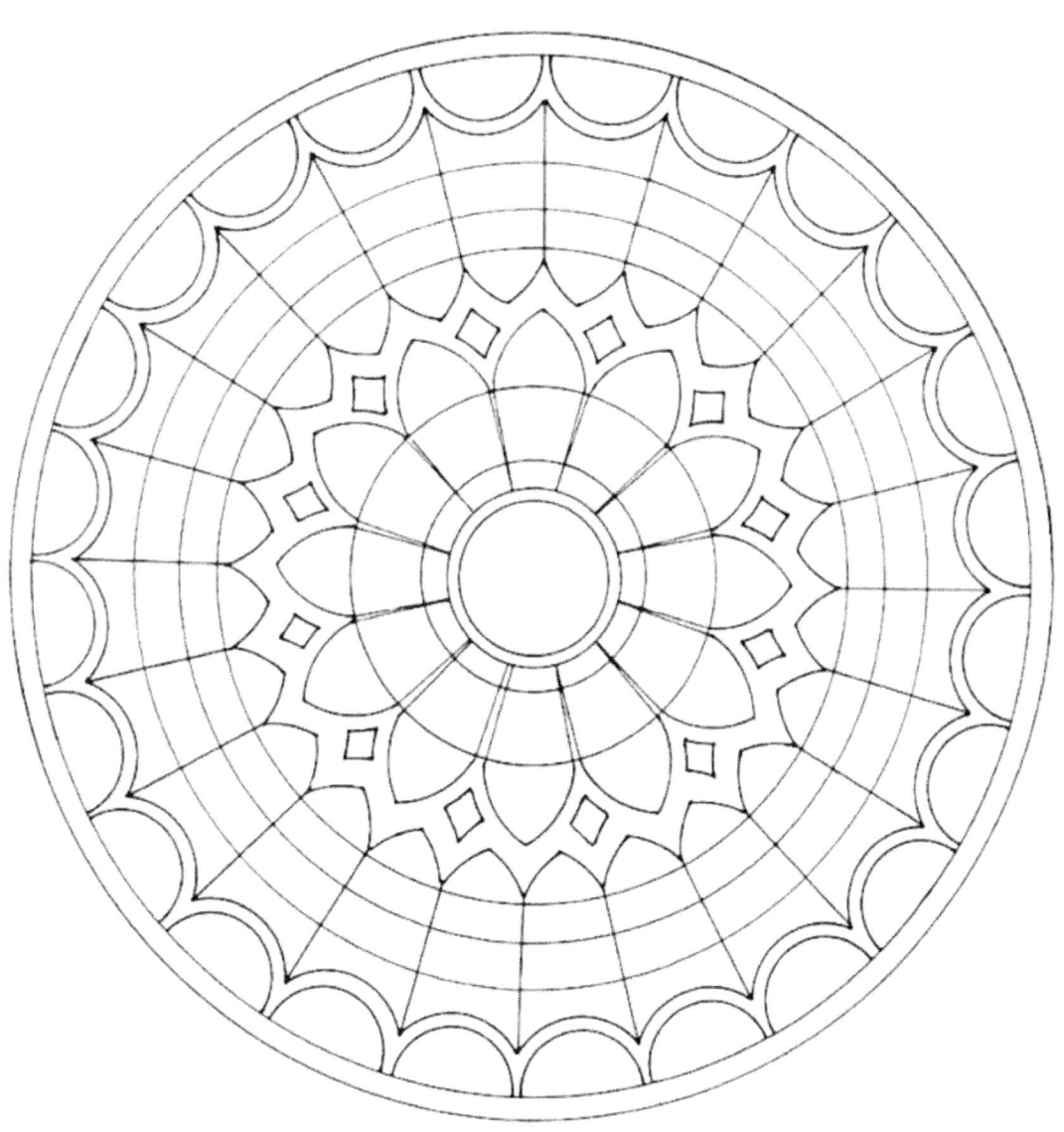

Circle 19

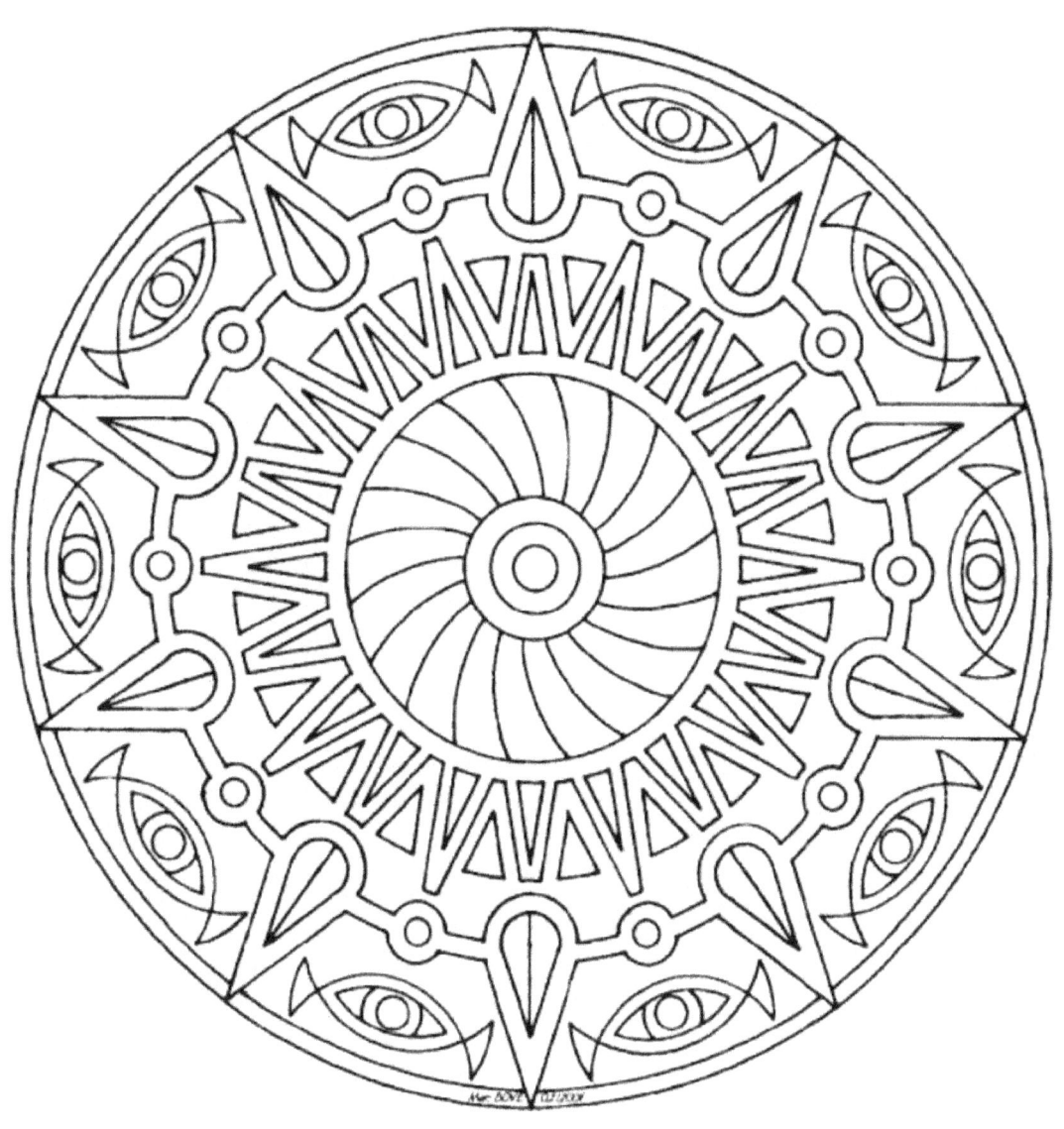

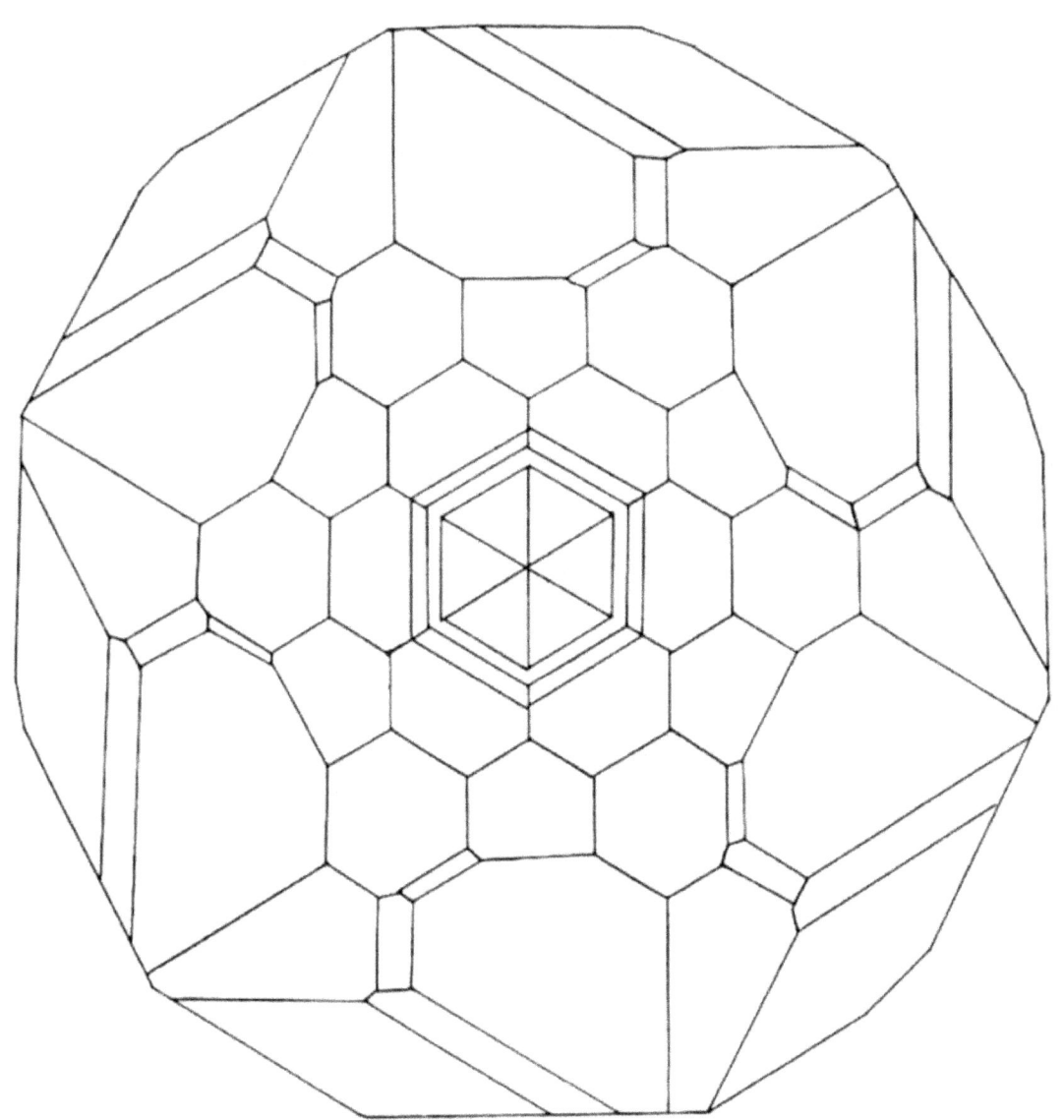

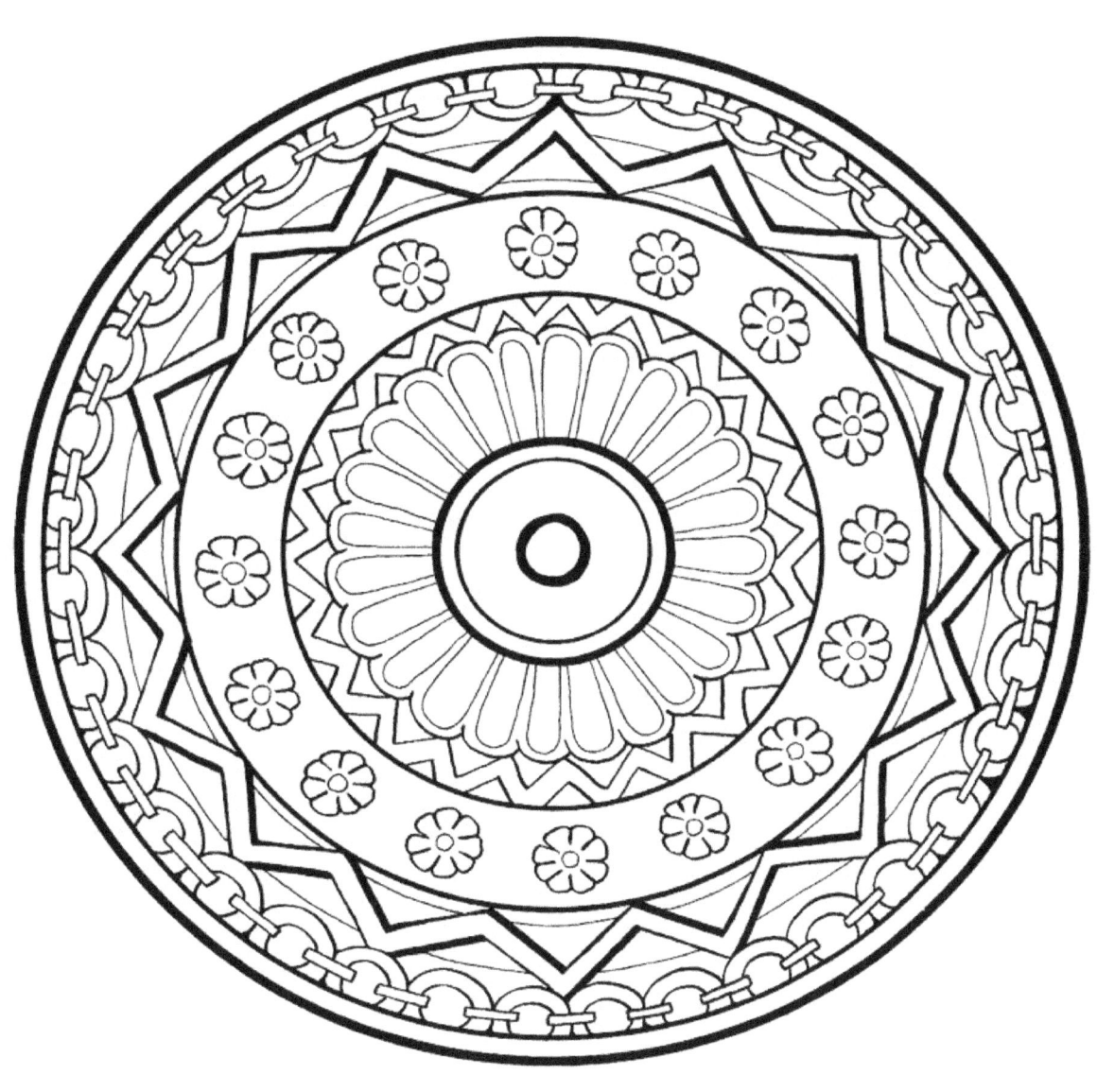

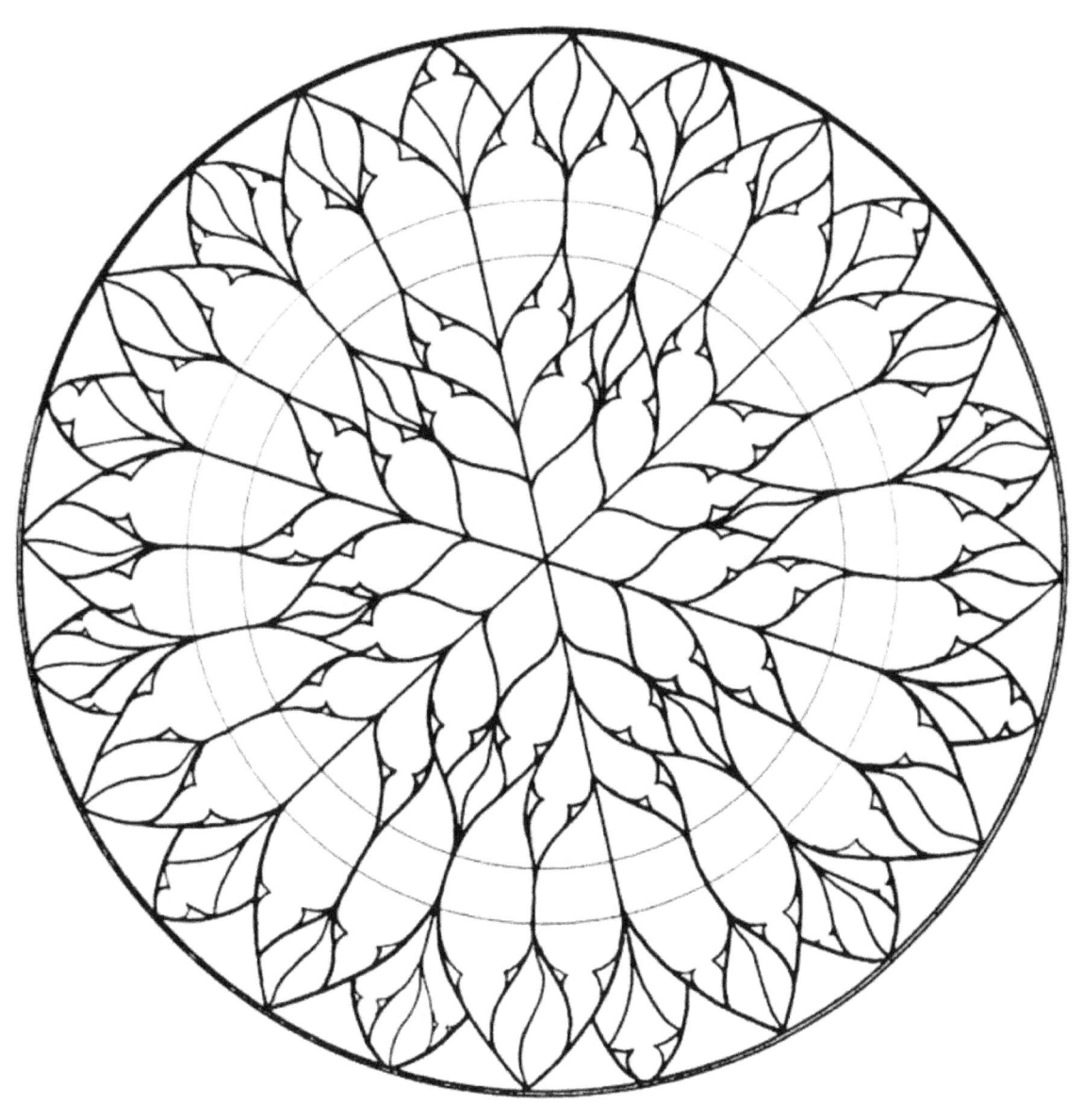

Square 1

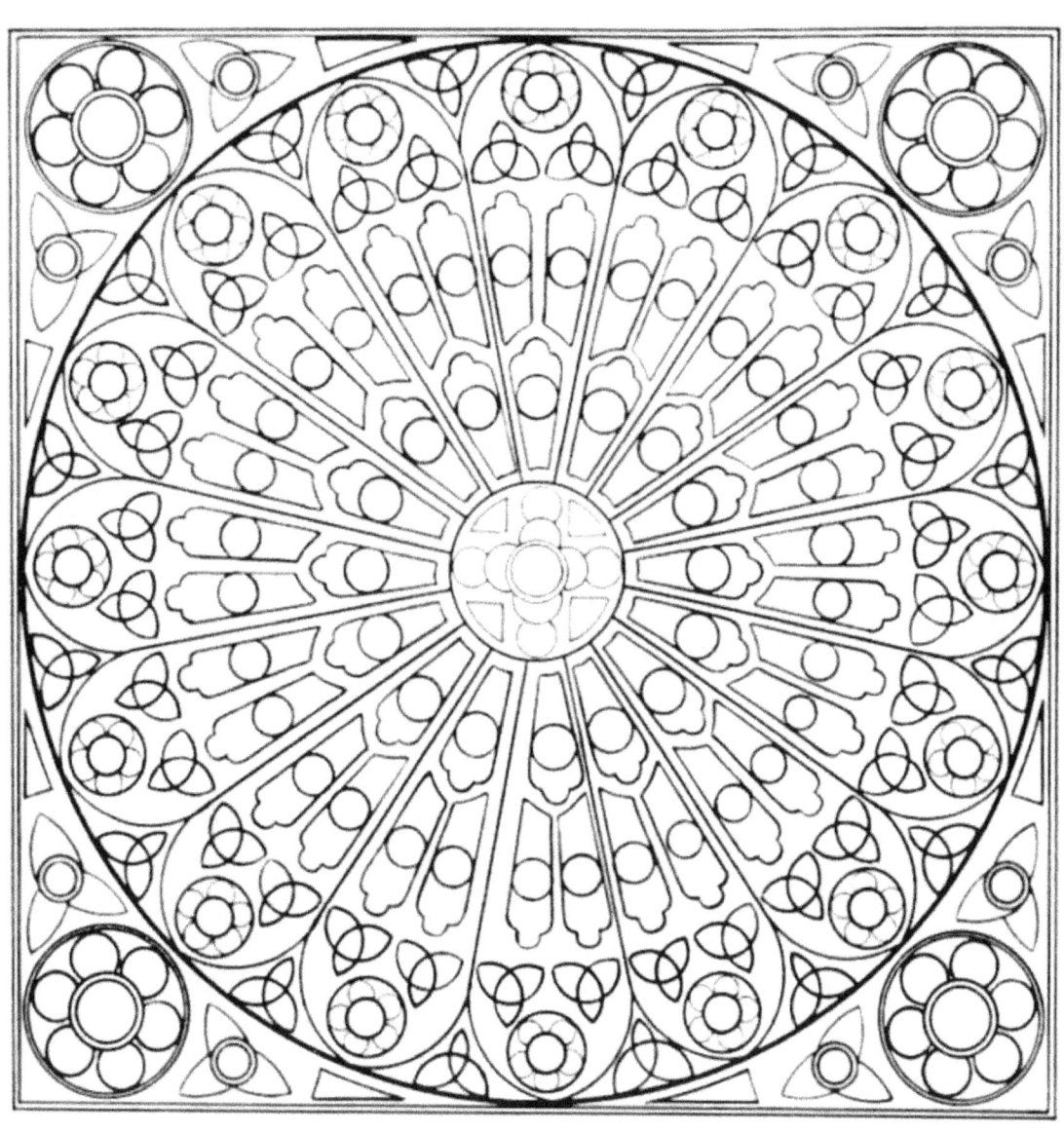

Circle 23

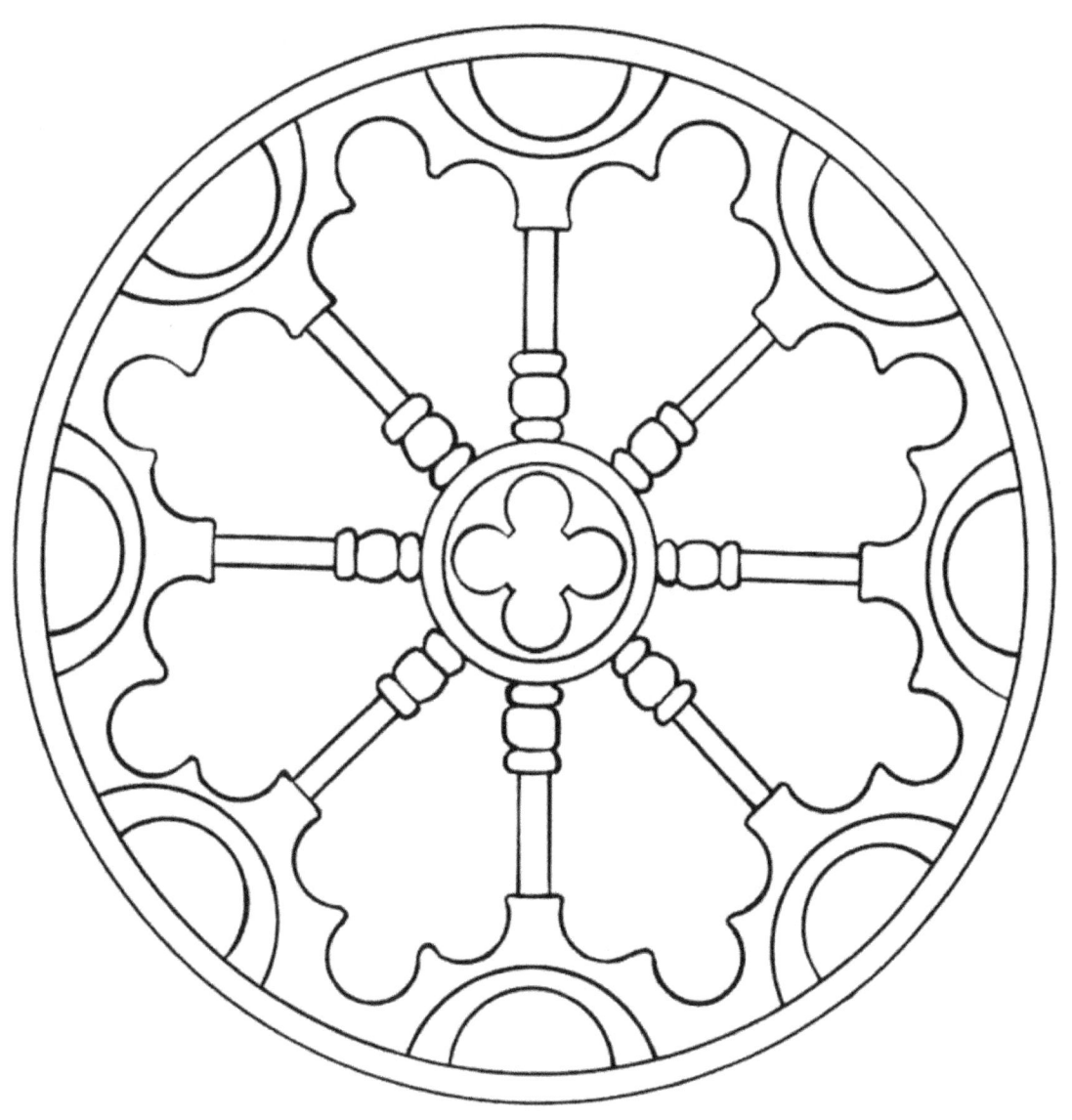

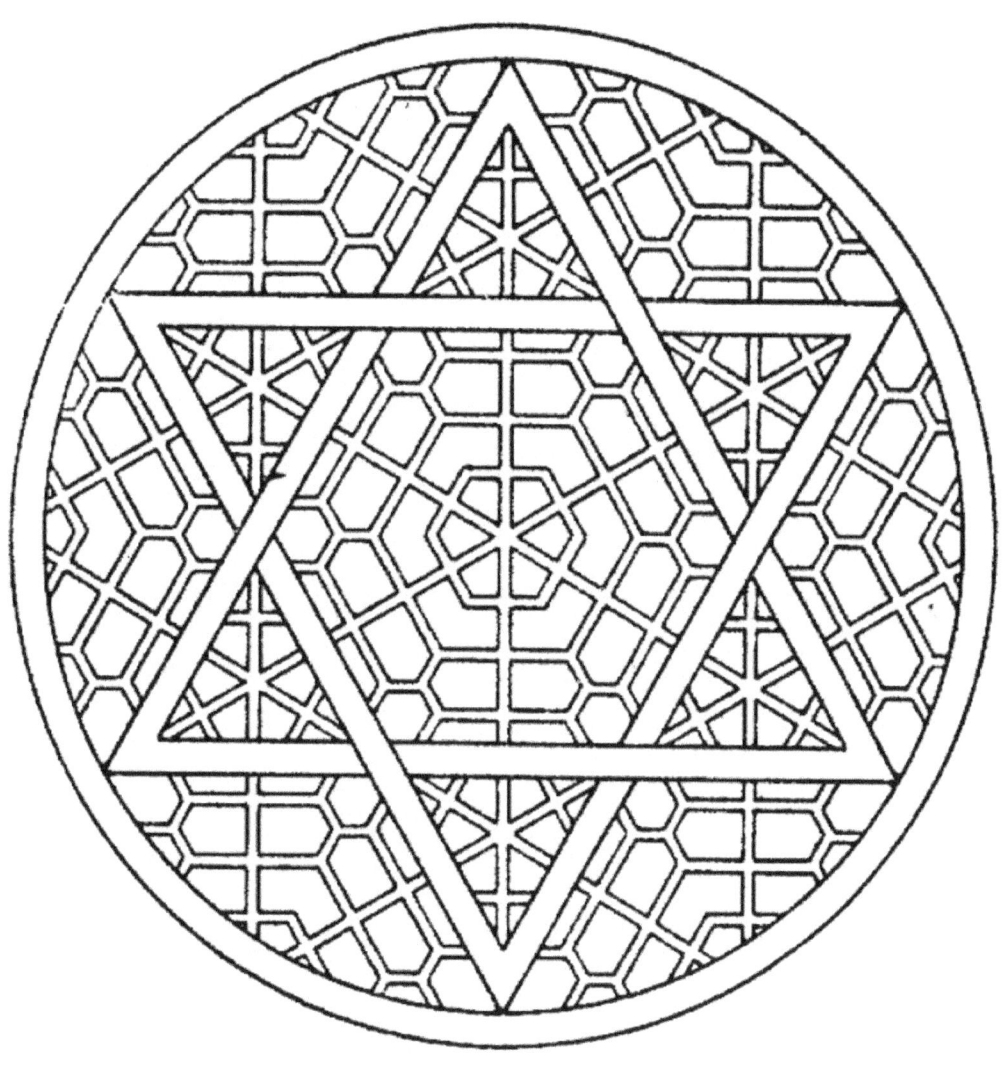

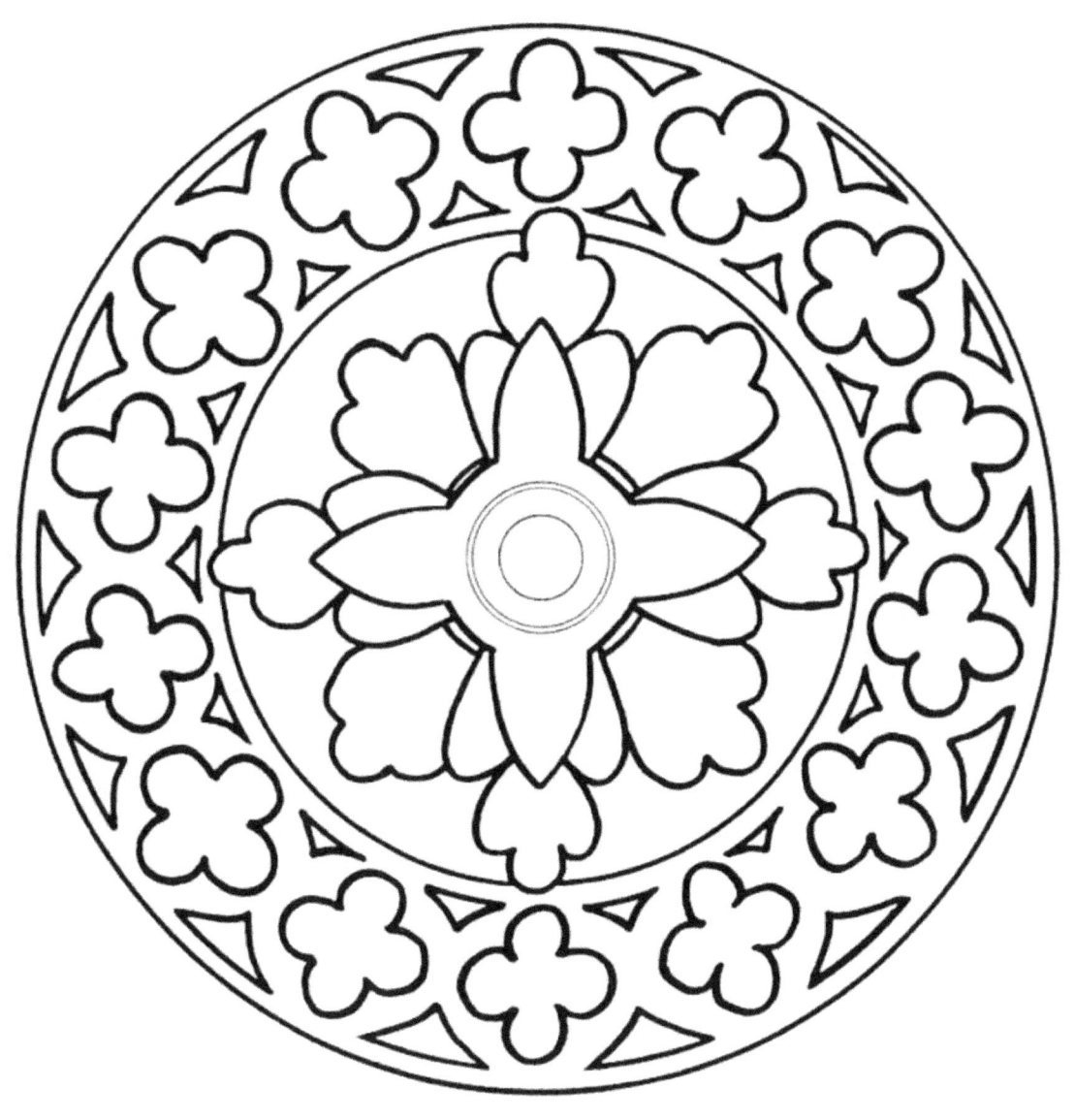

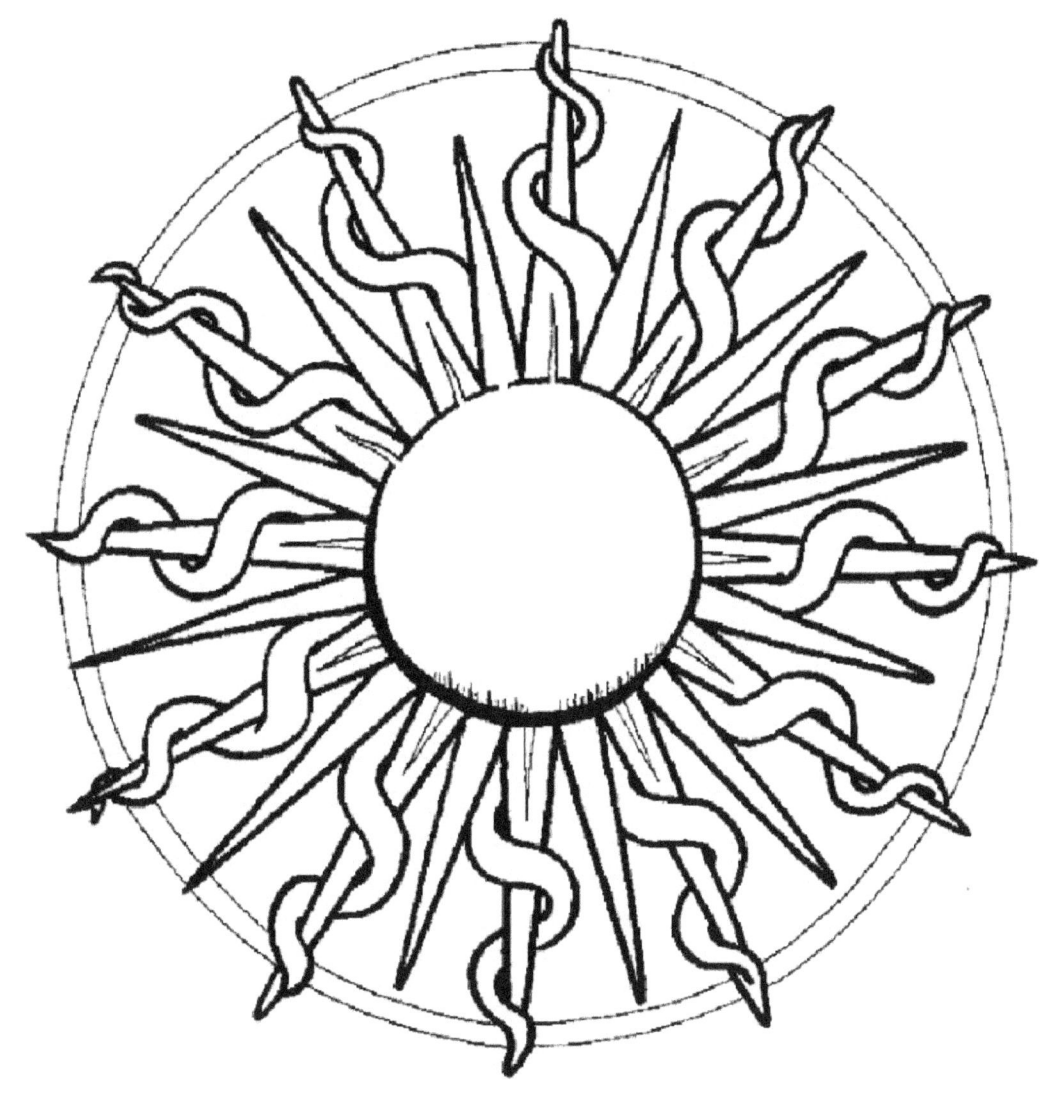

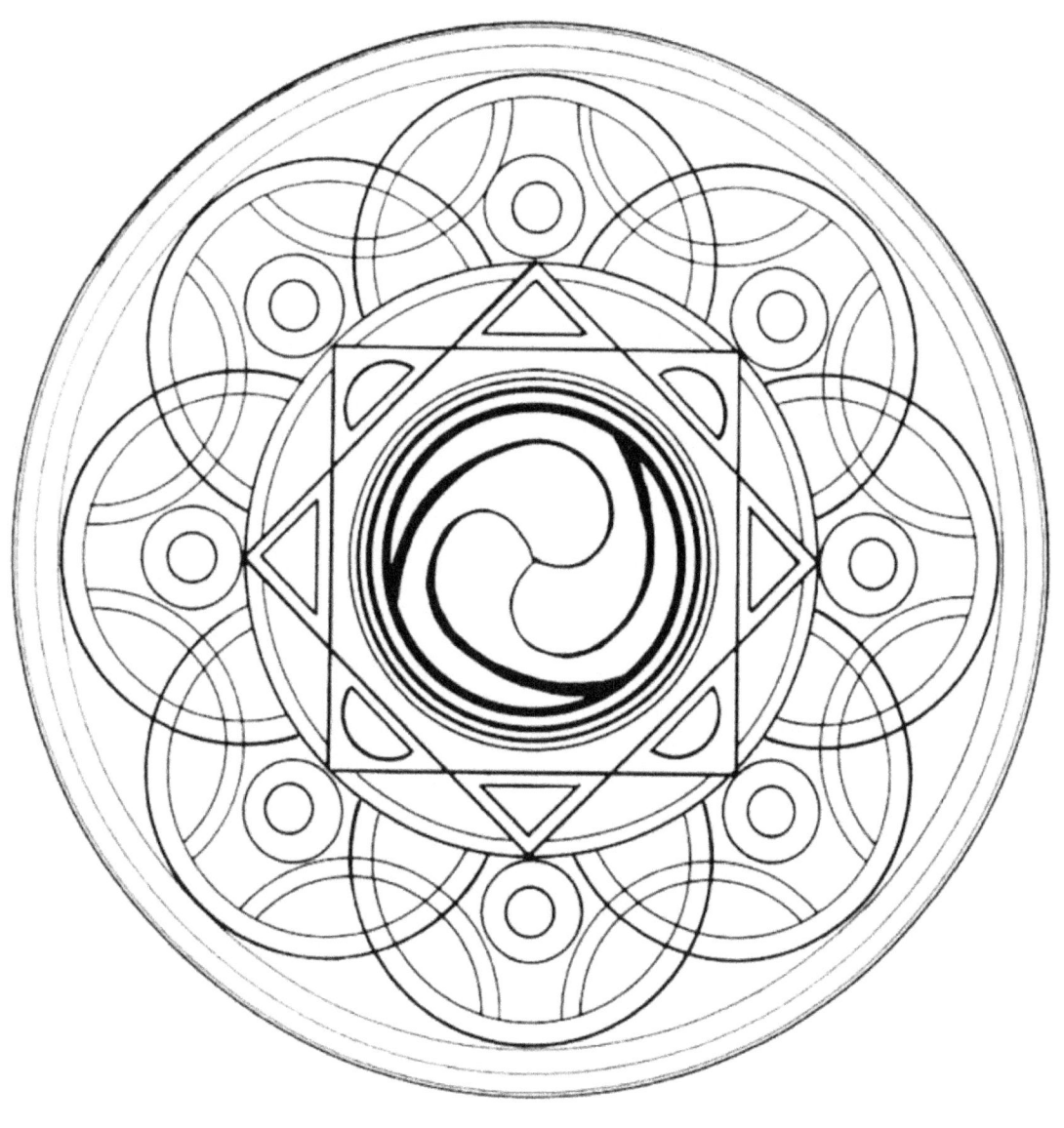

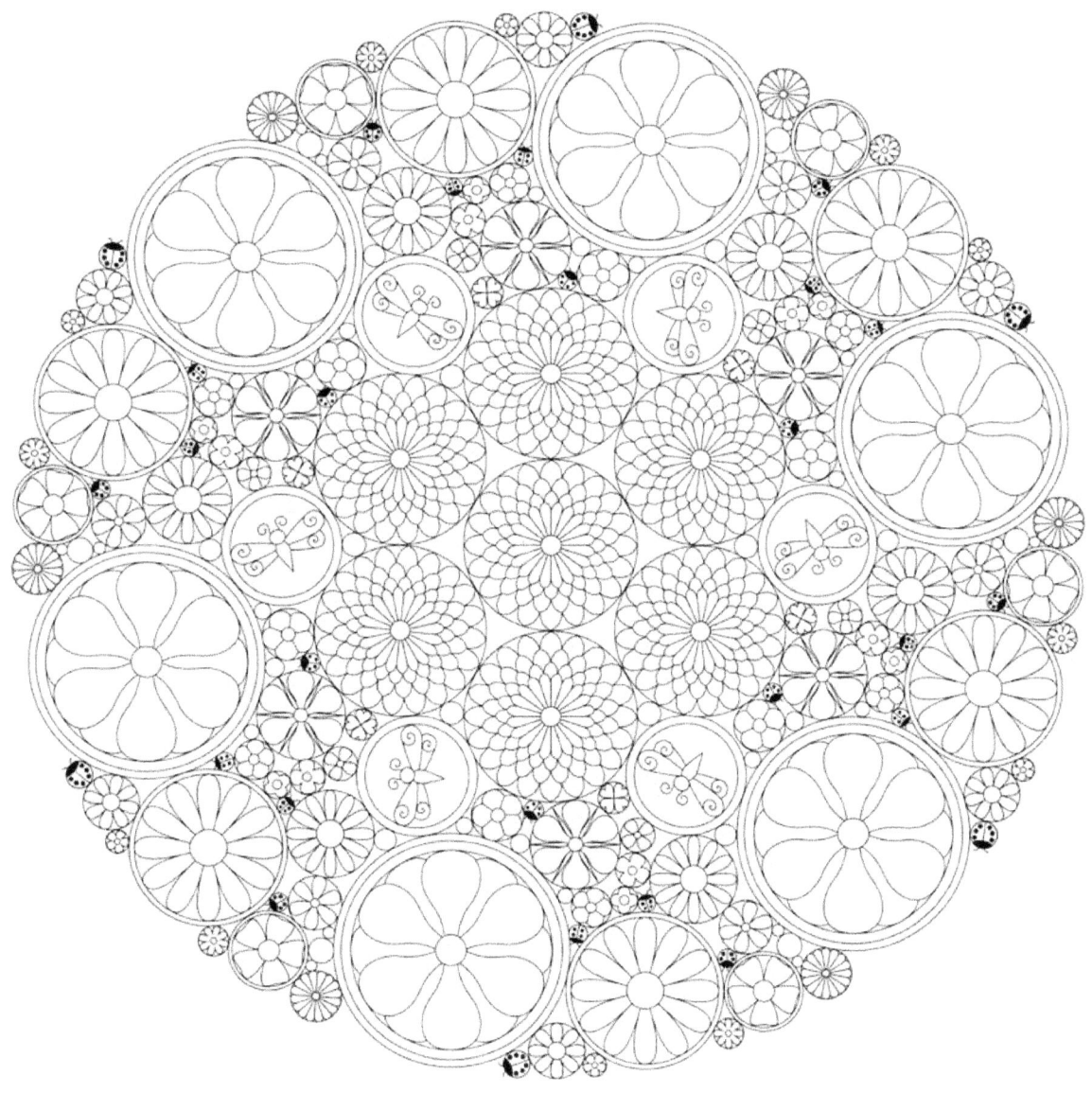

Circle 29

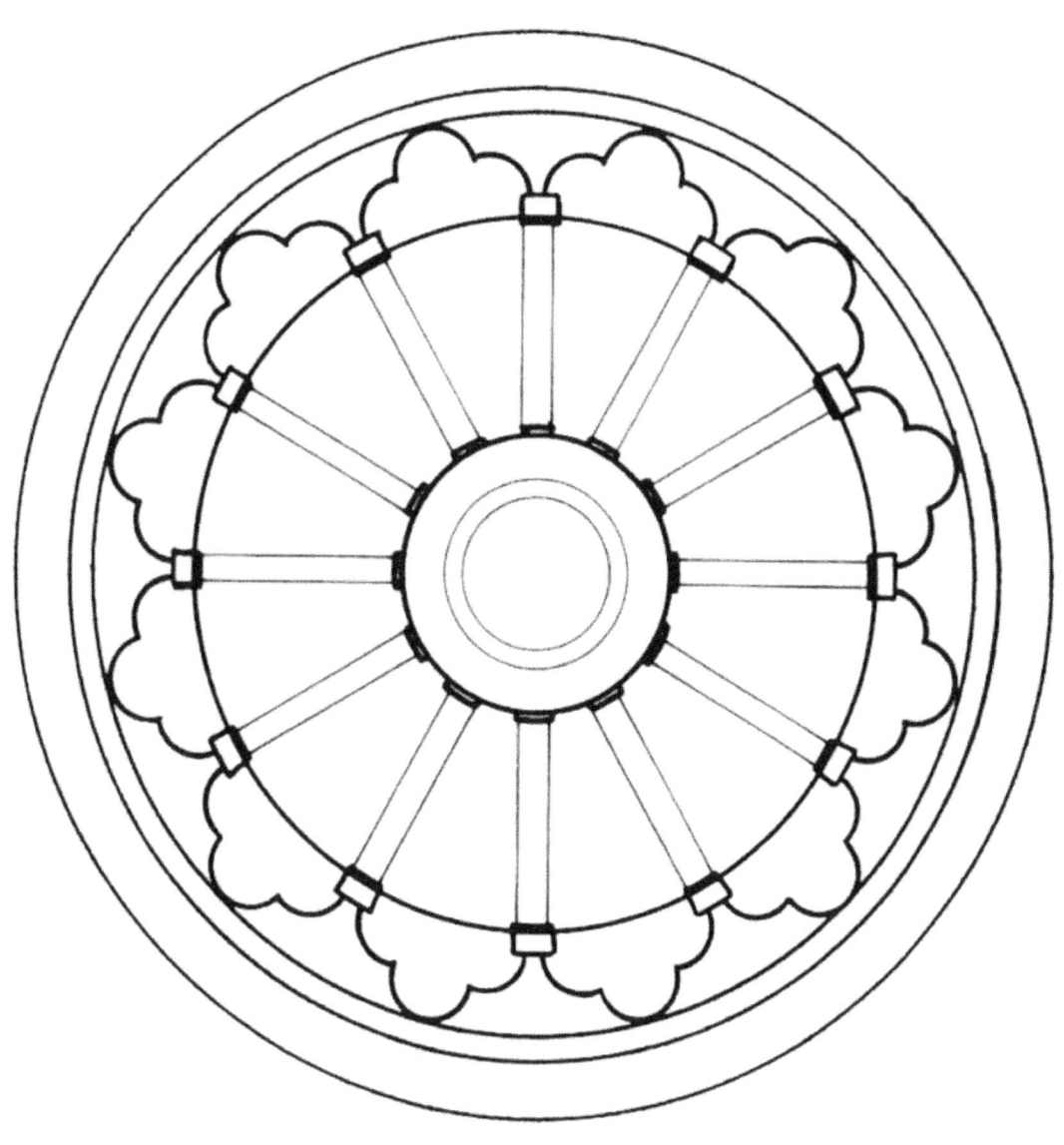

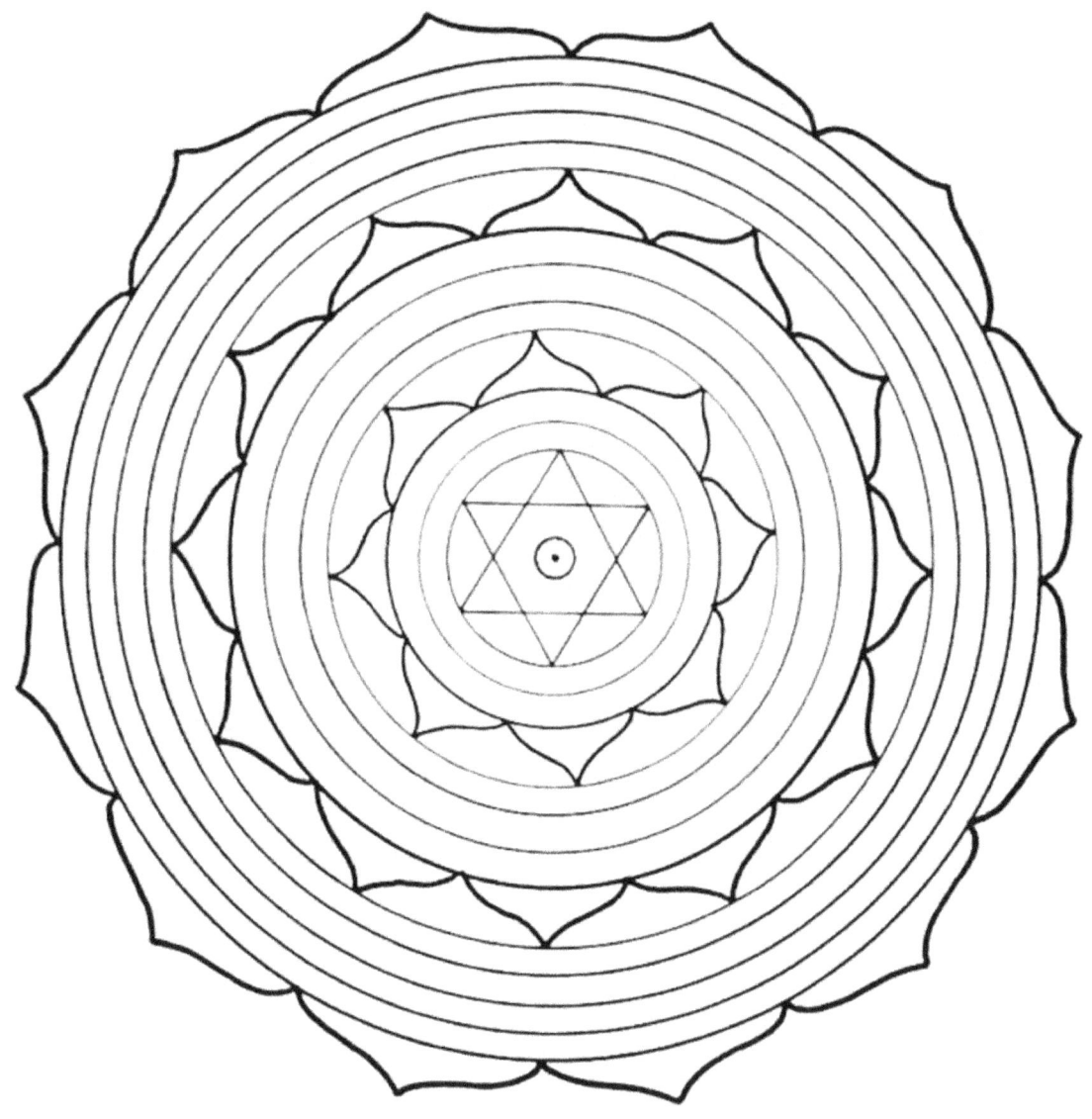

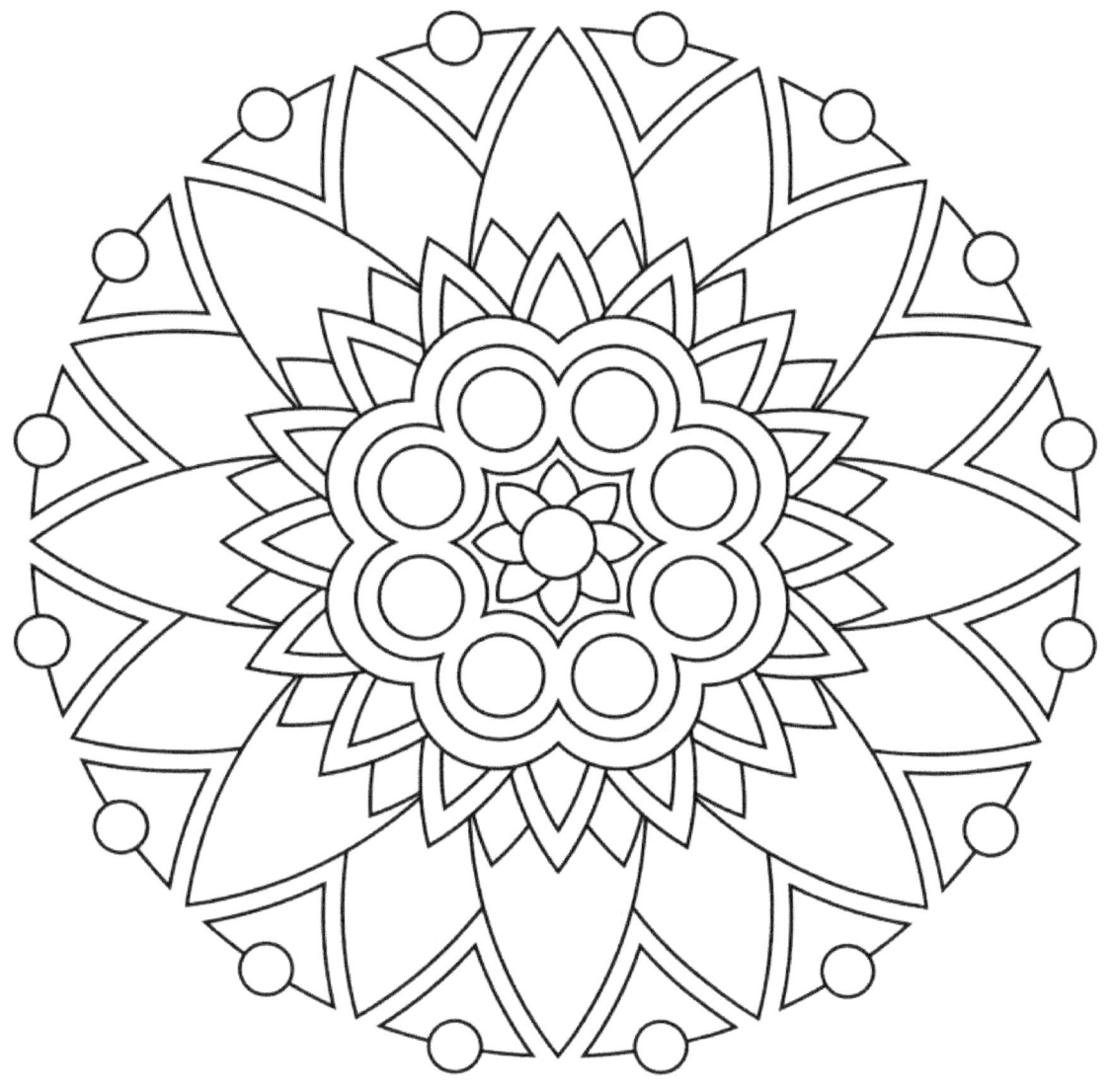

Square 2

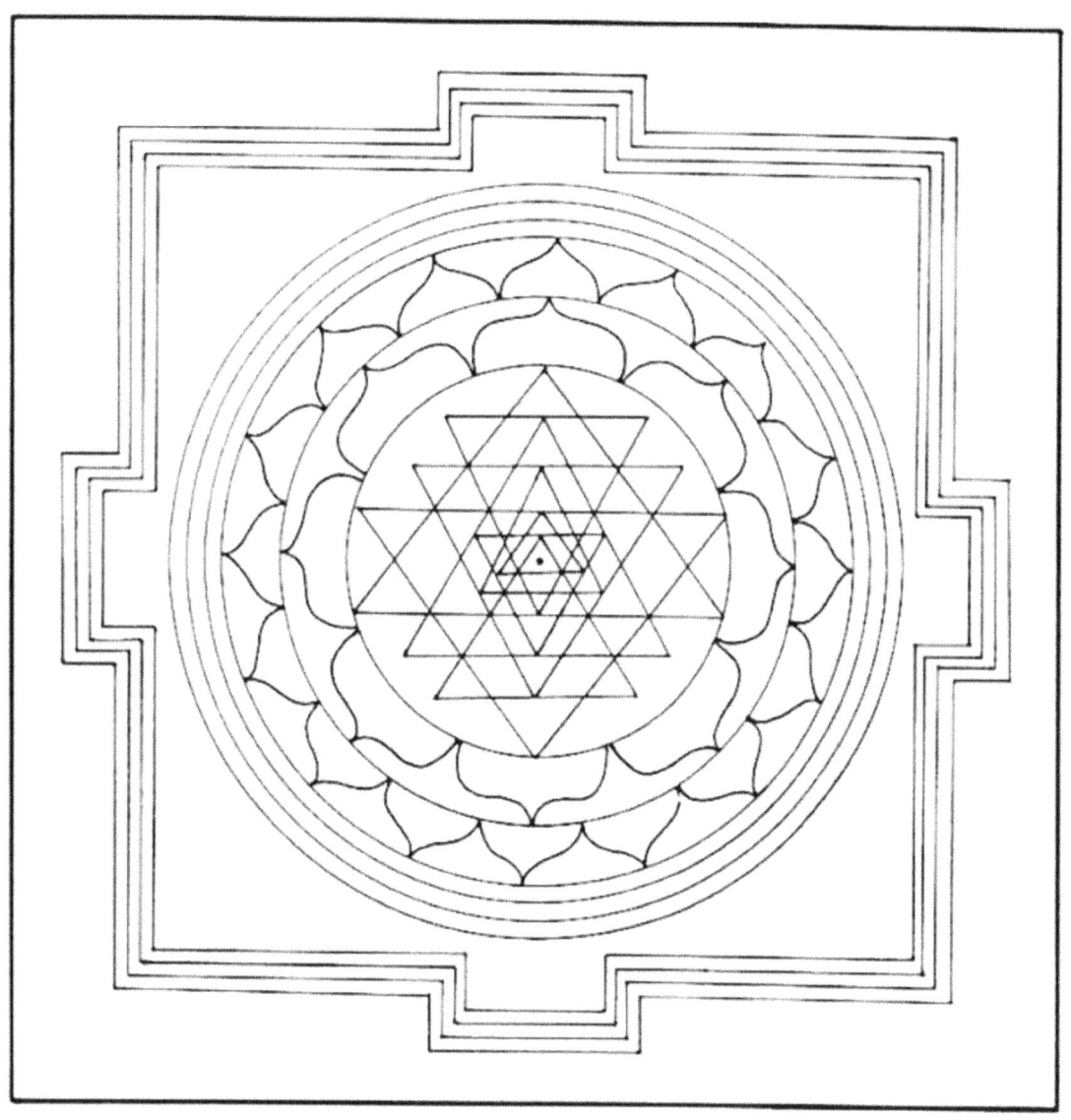

Circle 32

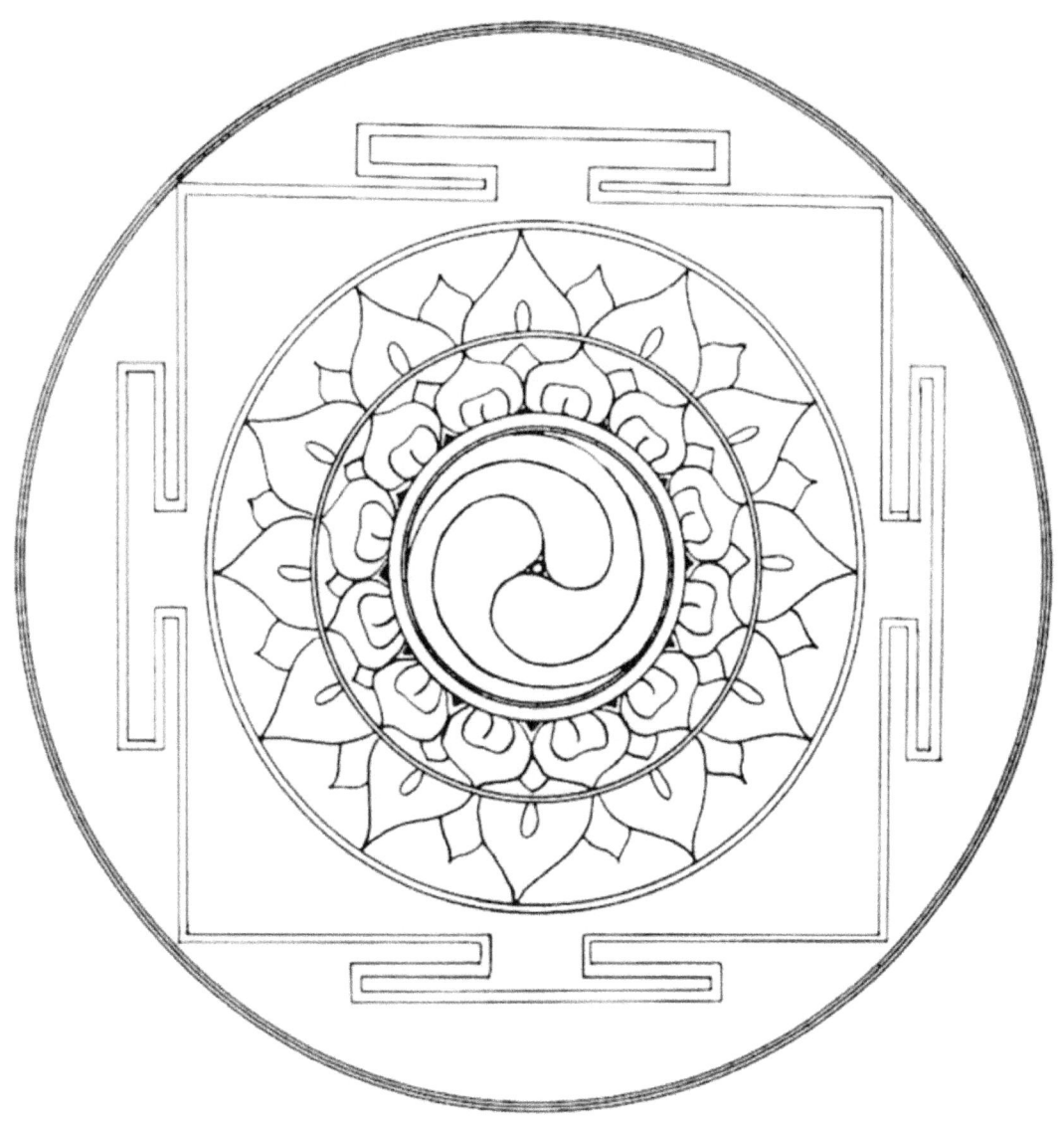

Octagon 1

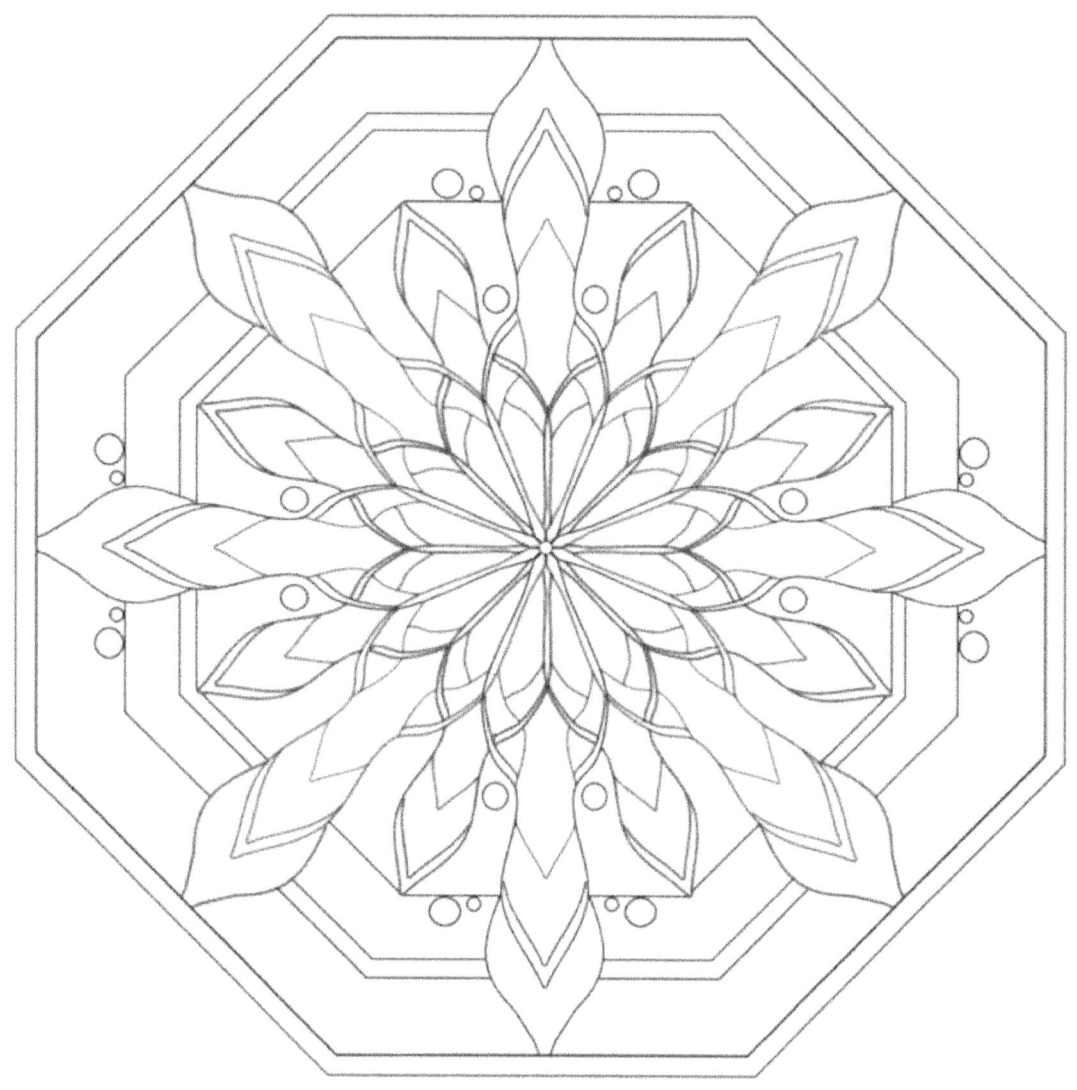

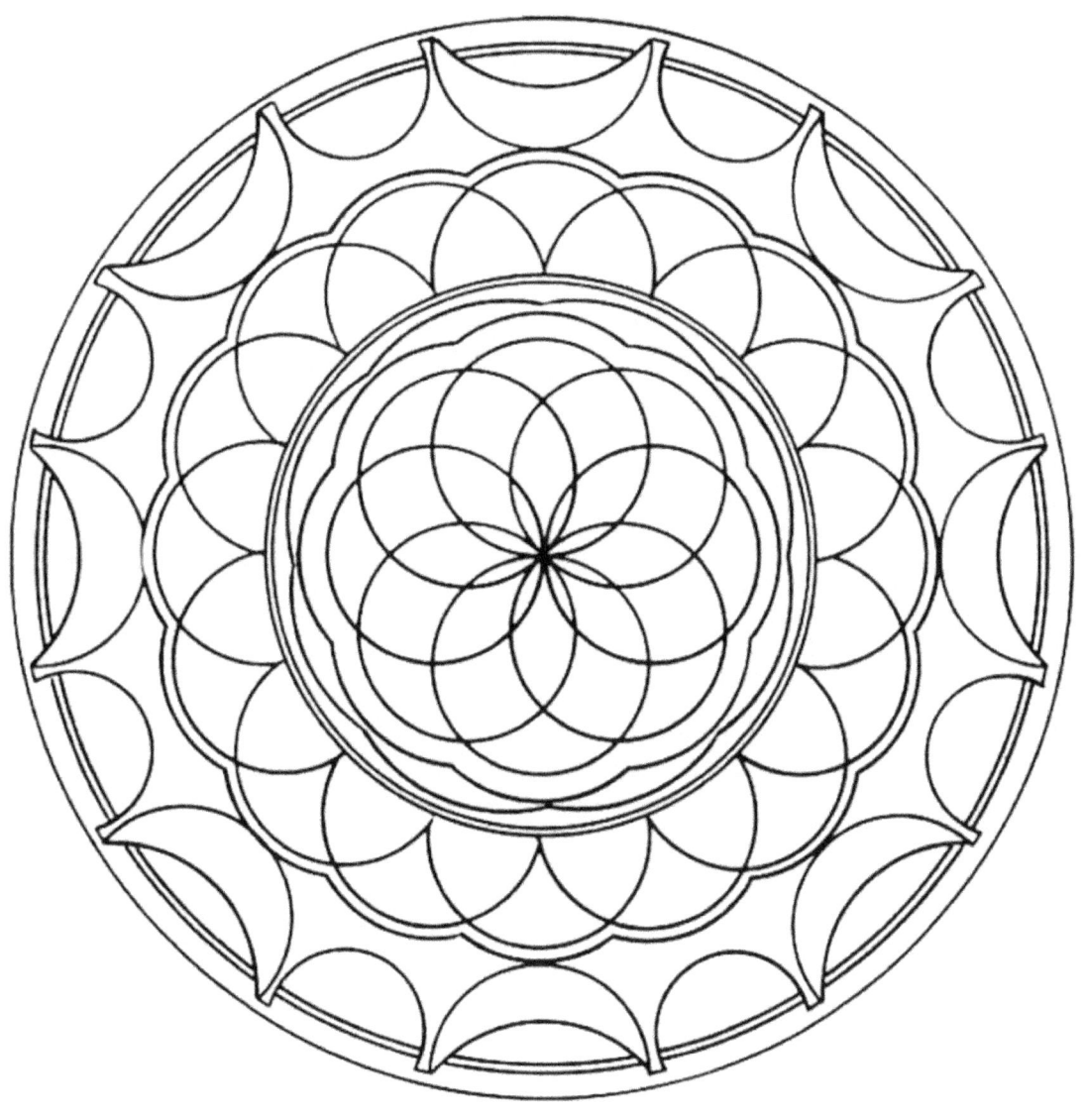

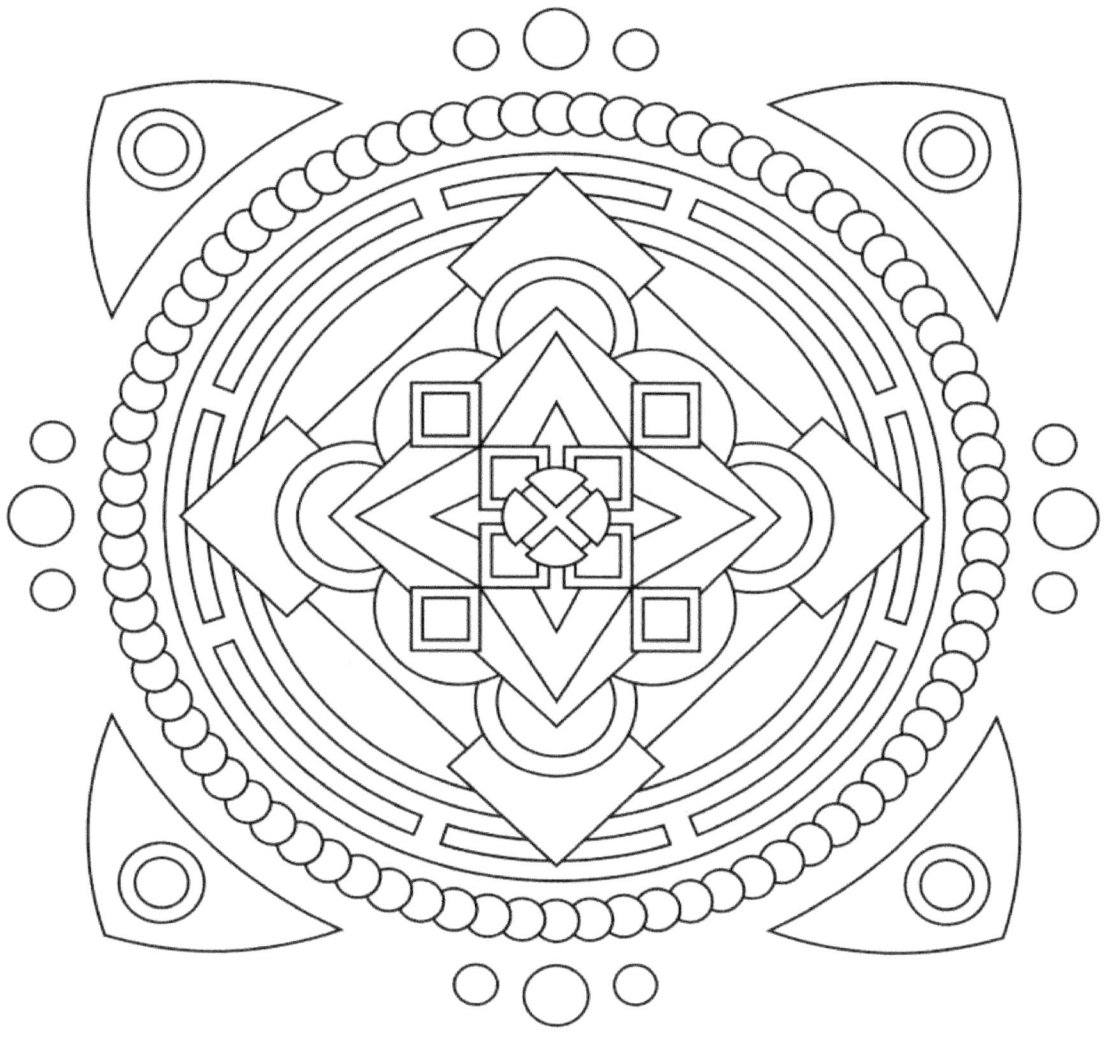

Octagon 2

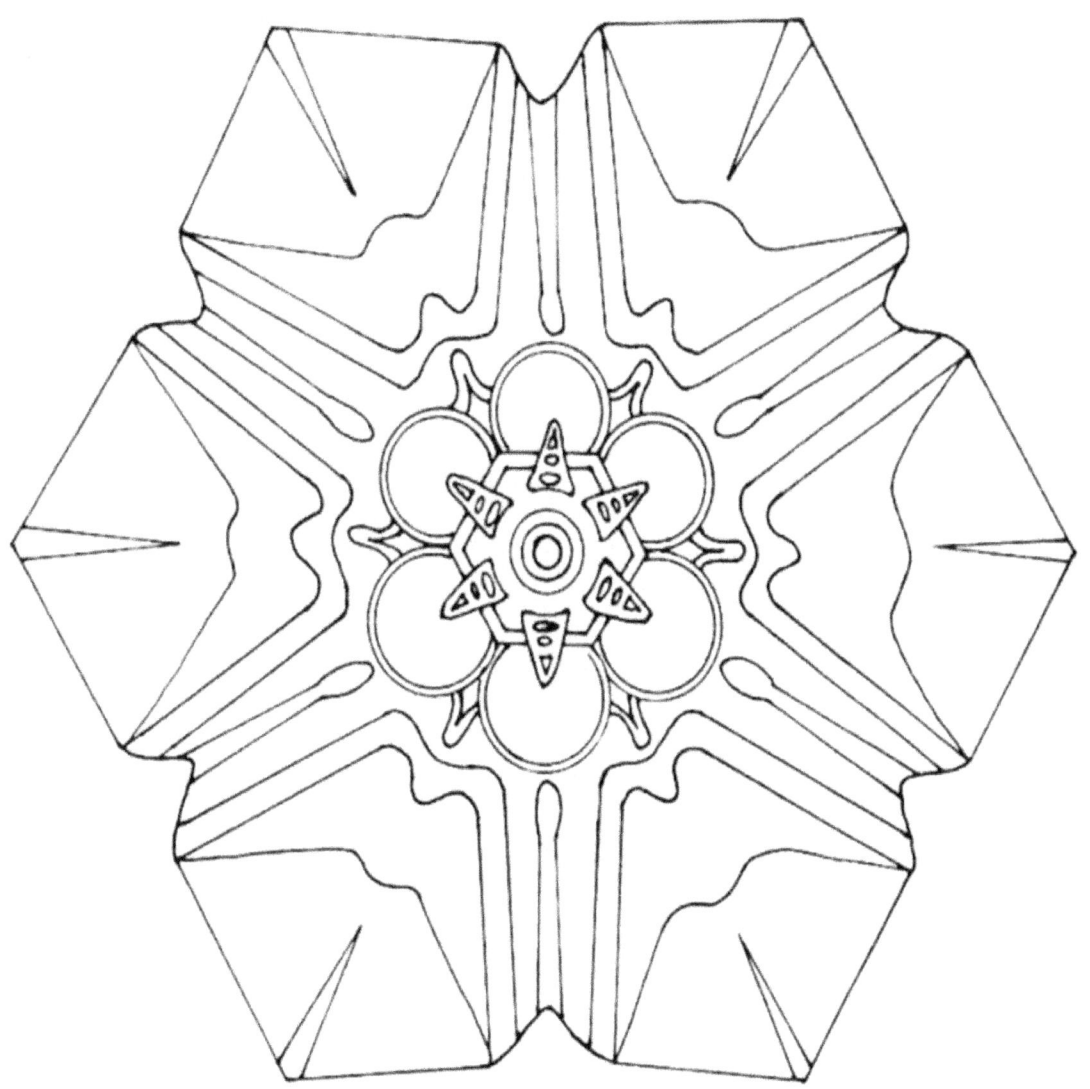

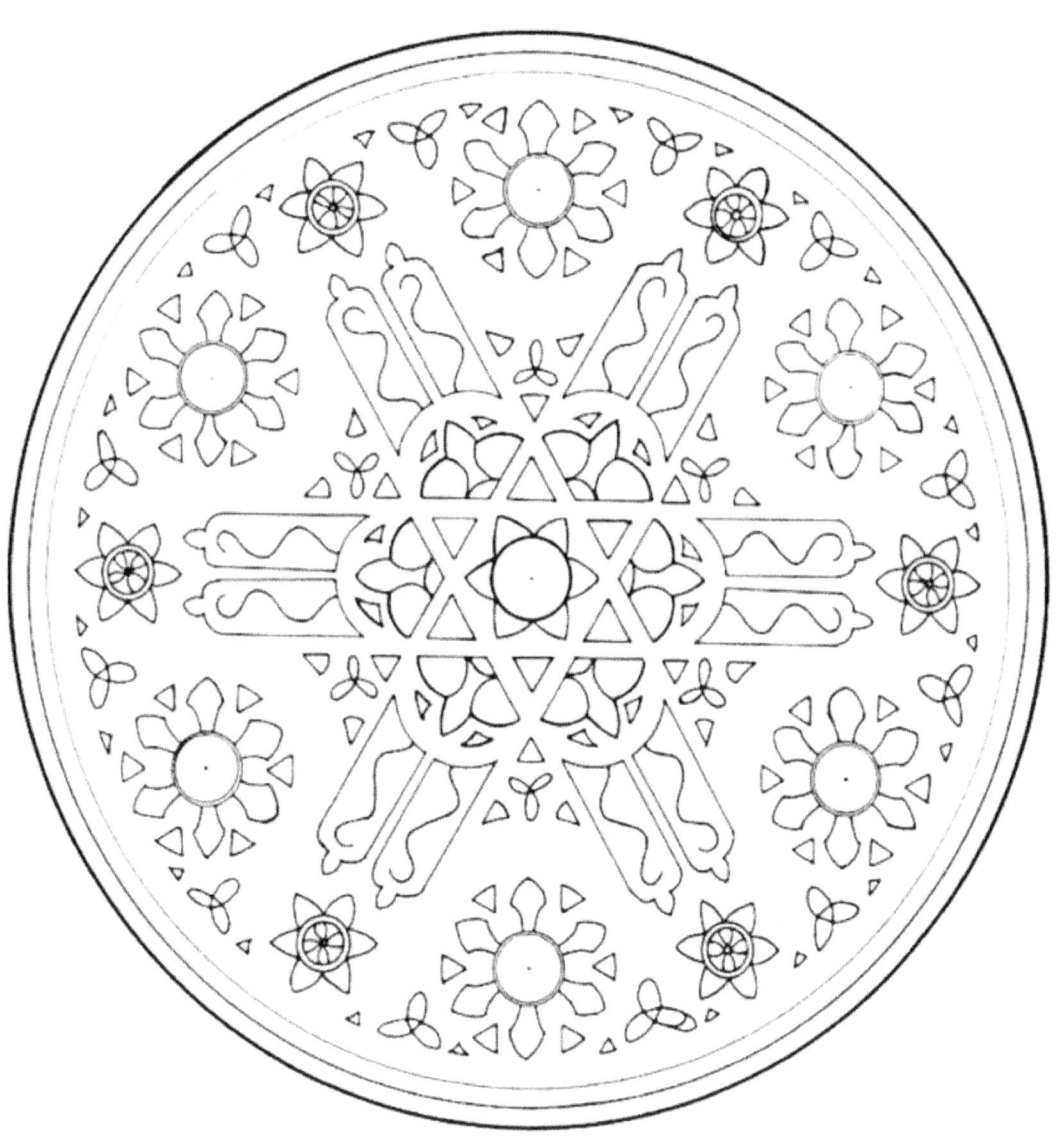

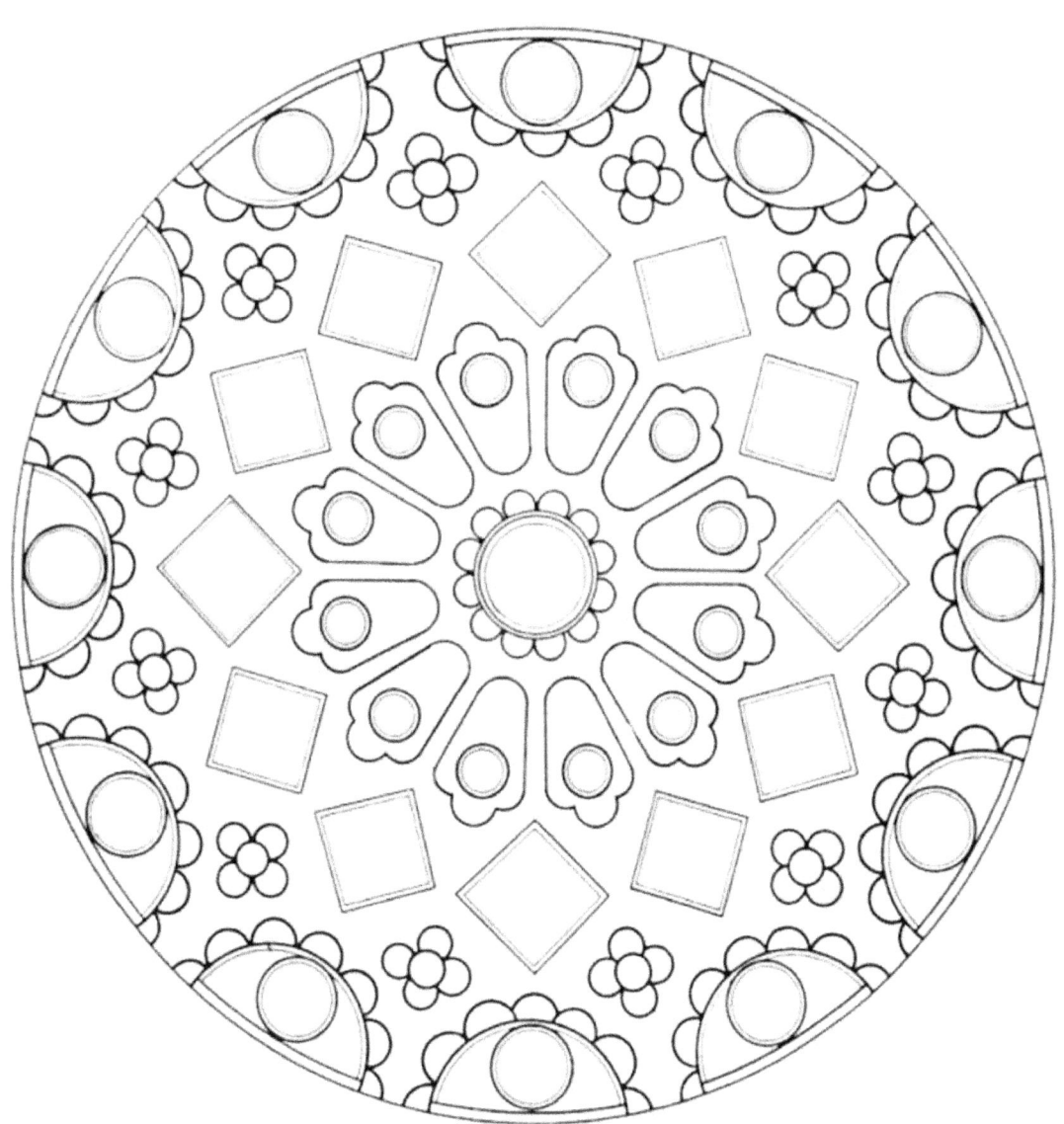

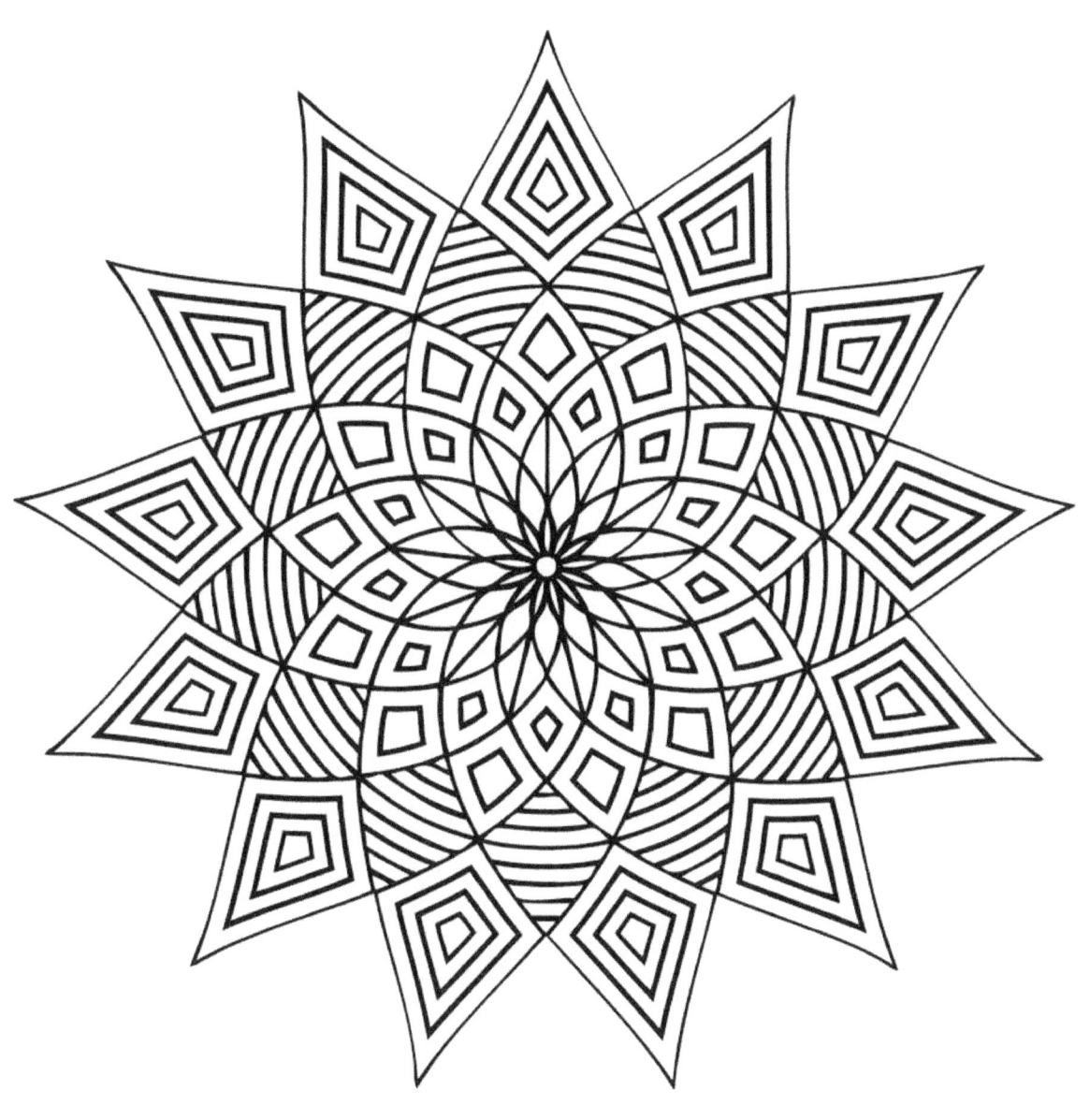

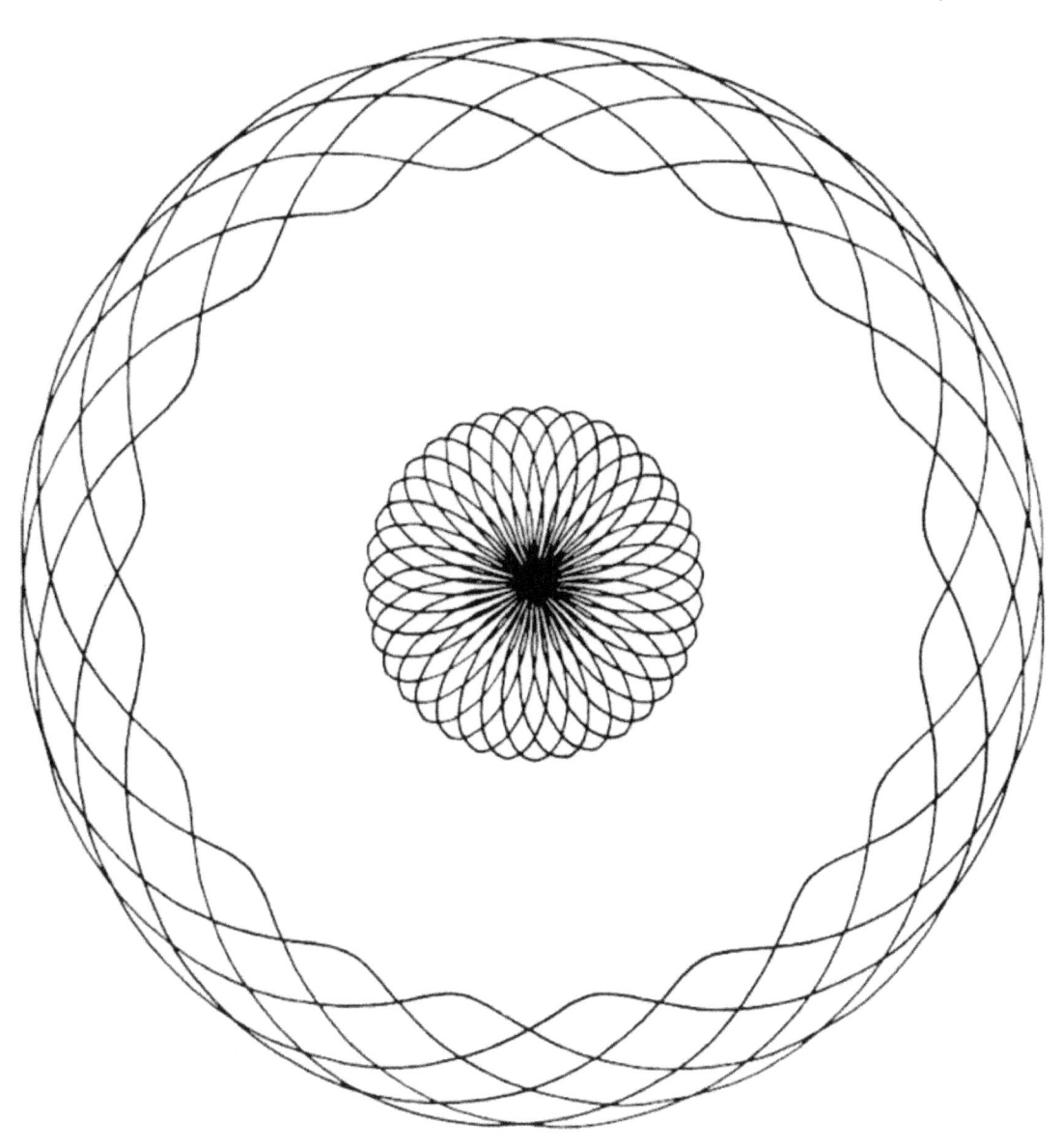

Cat 1

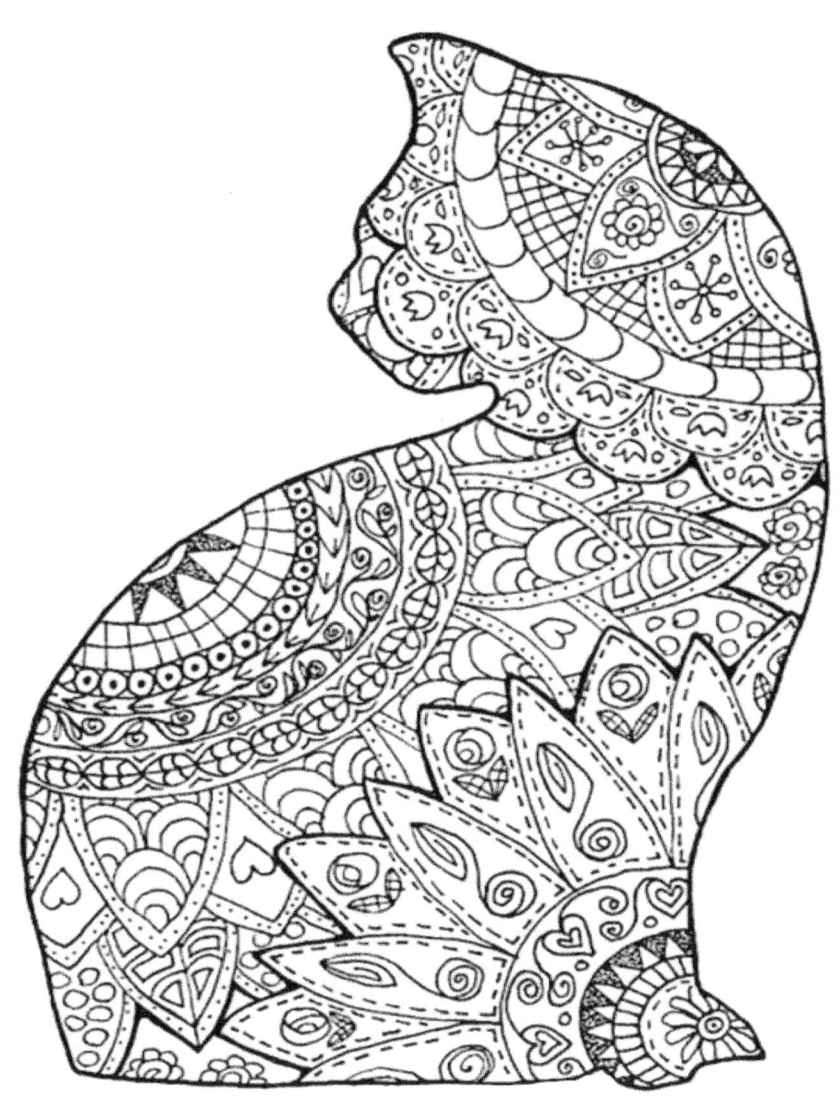

Circle 38

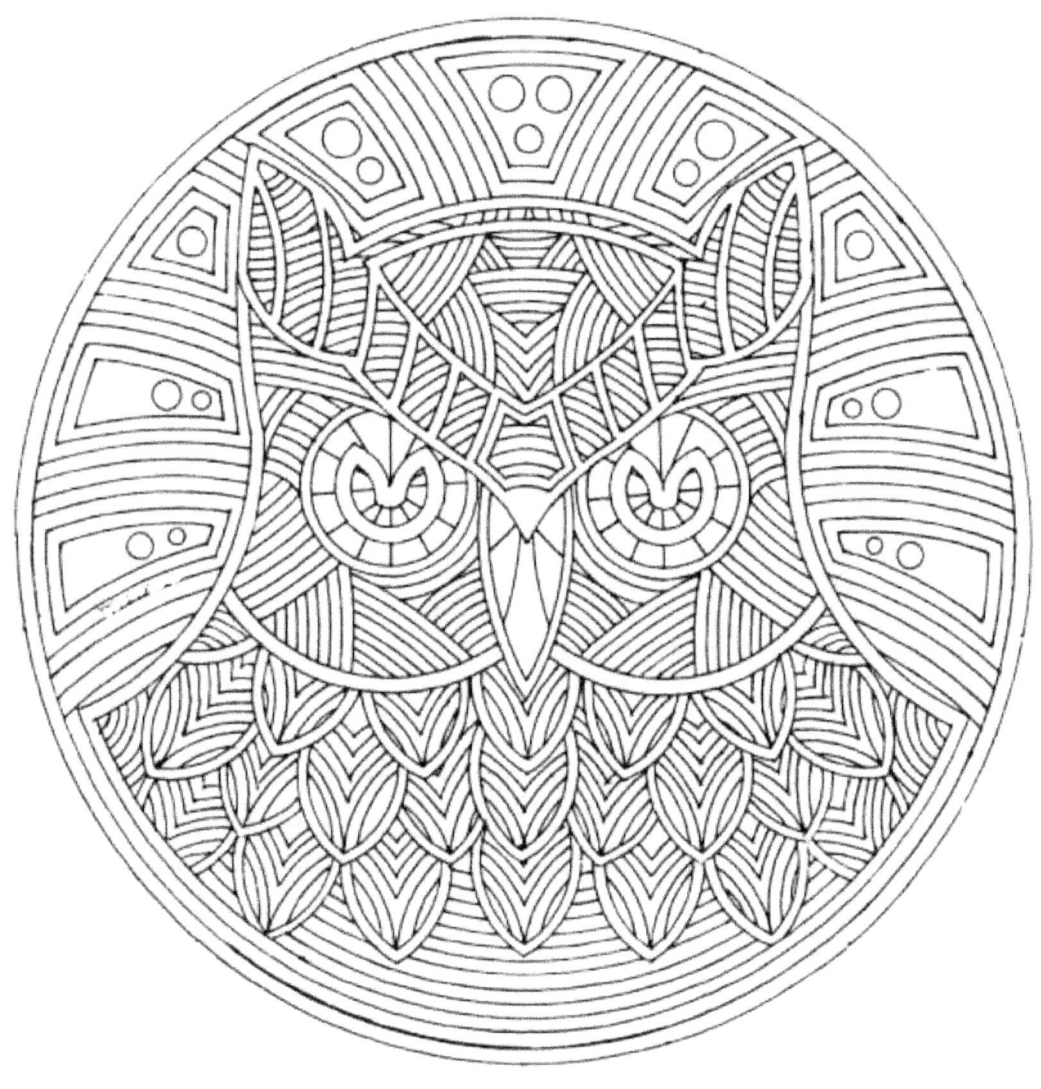

According to art therapist and mental health counselor Susanne F. Fincher, we owe the re-introduction of Mandalas into modern western thought to Carl Jung, the Swiss psychoanalyst. In his pioneering exploration of the unconscious through his own art making, Jung observed the motif of the circle spontaneously appearing. The circle drawings reflected his inner state at that moment. Familiarity with the philosophical writings of India prompted Jung to adopt the word "Mandala" to describe these circle drawings he and his patients made. In his autobiography, Jung wrote:

"I sketched every morning in a notebook a small circular drawing, which seemed to correspond to my inner situation at the time... Only gradually did I discover what the Mandalas really are: the Self, the wholeness of the personality, which if all goes well is harmonious."

— *Carl Jung, Memories, dreams, reflections*

Jung recognized that the urge to make Mandalas emerges during moments of intense personal growth. Their appearance indicates a profound re-balancing process is underway in the psyche. The result of the process is a more complex and better integrated personality.

"The Mandalas serve a conservative purpose—namely, to restore a previously existing order. But it also serves the creative purpose of giving expression and form to something that does not yet exist, something new and unique... The process is that of the ascending spiral, which grows upward while simultaneously returning again and again to the same point."

— *Jungian analyst Marie-Louise von Franz, C. G. Jung; Man and His Symbol*

Creating Mandalas helps stabilize, integrate, and re-order inner life.

According to the psychologist David Fontana, its symbolic nature can help one "to access progressively deeper levels of the unconscious, ultimately assisting the meditators to experience a mystical sense of oneness with the ultimate unity from which the cosmos in all its manifold forms arises.

www.ingramcontent.com/pod-product-compliance
Lightning Source LLC
Chambersburg PA
CBHW080710190526

45169CB00006B/2322